The Other Side:

A Psychic's Story

By

David Drew

Ghost Writer Publications UK

COVER PHOTOGRAPH BY AYESHA DREW

PUBLISHED BY GHOST WRITER PUBLICATIONS UK

ISBN 978-1-5272-0617-5

ILLUSTRATIONS

AND COVER PHOTOGRAPH

BY

AYESHA DREW

www.ayeshadrew.com

Contents

Foreword
By Ricky Tomlinson

I first met David Drew Many years ago. I had at that time, a bistro/bar in Liverpool called 'The Limelight', which faced the iconic Adelphi Hotel. It had previously been a 'gentleman's club', but had been empty for many years and required quite a lot of renovation. All sorts of people came there, some to perform, others for a drink or a game of pool. We even opened early in the morning during the postman's strike to serve tea and breakfast to the striking workers.

At first, small things would happen there. Strange noises would be heard at night, but not much notice was taken as the lads would be too busy laughing or playing pool. This was soon to change.

One of our regular customers was known as 'The Garstang Butterfly' because of two butterflies tattooed on her ankles. She had been a lady of the night in her younger years, and she fascinated me with tales of her exploits, such as being thrown overboard into the Mersey after being abused by foreign seamen docked in Liverpool. It was because of this lady, who I prefer to call Chloe, that I met David Drew.

One evening in The Limelight, Chloe said, "Rick, I've had a really bad night, I need to go home." Usually I would drive her or ask one of my regulars to take her home in my car, but there was no-one there who could drive her, and I couldn't leave the bar, so I told her to go upstairs to my flat for a few hours' sleep and I would run her home after I shut up for the night. She took my keys for the flat and went upstairs. For an hour or two things went on as normal in the bar, lads playing pool or cards and chatting away as usual, but then a scream rang out from the rooms above. I dashed up the stairs to the flat, followed by two or three customers. Chloe had smashed the window and climbed out onto the parapet. We coaxed her in and asked what was wrong. She told us she had woken and moved to come downstairs, when a tall man in a cap and long overcoat wouldn't let her pass. He said, "I'm waiting for Nelly", then disappeared just before we arrived. A day or two after the story was printed in the newspaper, David came to the Limelight and had a look around. For three days he trawled through the building. He was living in Llandudno so he stayed in a hotel next to the bar for three days and nights at his own expense. Finally he said to me, "Rick, the place is alive with ghosts." How right he was proven to be! This was only the first of many experiences in the club.

He went about his work, sometimes not even stopping for a cup of tea. I left it to him until the end of the third day when he said to me, "I have to sort this last one out, then everything should be okay." I didn't understand what he meant, but he went into the upstairs bathroom and was there for what seemed like an age. When he finally came out I thought he had been fighting a world champion! He was red in the face and his hair was dishevelled. "It's all clear now," he said, "you won't be bothered again." I asked him what had happened and he explained that a spirit had shot his mate, then committed suicide, but was refusing to 'go over'.

David left after three days, but we stayed in touch. Sometimes I even introduced him onto stage. He obviously has a special gift. This may sound like a load of nonsense to people who don't believe, but since then I have never had a single doubt in the existence of the spirit world. It is not something we should be afraid of. Perhaps this book will let us in on some of David's secrets, of which there must be many.

Preface

Poor health has compelled me to retire, and I find myself with time on my hands and no plausible excuse not to write the autobiography I was asked to deliver ten years ago.

Lacking any fear of death, I have spent a lifetime smoking to excess, completely overlooking the possibility that dying was not the only potential consequence of my actions. As my physical condition deteriorates, I regularly reflect on my life as David Drew, and hope and pray daily that I have done enough. Each earthly life passes in the blink of an eye and I long to make this final mark on a world I must surely leave behind.

Brain and pen willing, I have all that I need to at last share with you a treasure chest of memories and mysteries. An echo of this life if you will, before I move on to the next.

All stories are true. I have changed some names and locations to protect the anonymity of the people that hold them dear.

Introduction

We are all here for a purpose, some to learn, some to teach and most of us do a little of both. As a child, I didn't know the reason for my having this life. How could I? As a rule, we don't discover our purpose until long after we pass over, and by then of course, it's too late to undo all the mistakes that lured us off our intended path. In short, the not knowing was nothing unusual. What is unusual is that in a quite unique turn of events I did subsequently come to learn the reason for my life whilst I was still living it.

I was born with a variety of psychic abilities rarely found stuffed into one person. It is my belief that most people have one or more of these gifts dormant within them, but with me, they came ready to rumble as part of the package. A free gift, whether I liked it or not. No substitutions, exchanges or refunds.

In this aspect you and I differ perhaps, but in most respects you will find we are just the same. I enjoy fish and chips and football, I loathe and detest telesales calls and how I long for that beer at the end of a busy day to help me unwind.

And you? You have had that feeling of being somewhere before. You occasionally know who is calling before you pick up the phone and didn't you, just for a second, catch sight of a shadowy figure in the corner of your eye? You see, we are more alike than you might think.

Everyone has the potential to nurture their dormant psychic senses. If you and I were to take piano lessons, I am sure with a bit of practice I could learn to bash out 'Three Blind Mice'. Maybe you would excel and go on to play the Albert Hall, but we would both have the potential to develop this talent to some degree or other. Similarly, everyone can use their psychic ability if they put their mind to it. For me it was not a choice. As a little boy who could see dead people, I would quite possibly have chosen differently.

1
Faces in the Dark

When I was a small boy, I had no idea that my memories of curling up cosy and cramped in the womb, or indeed of the wonders that came before that, were in any way unusual. I was oblivious to the reality that other people didn't see spirit on a daily basis the way I did. My family humoured me regarding my 'imaginary friends', and it came as a shock to all concerned when we realised that I was the one who had been telling the truth all these years and that their acknowledgements and interactions with these people had just been a kindly pretence for my benefit.

As the long shadow of my childhood fades, I am surprised to feel an ache for those days I had almost forgotten. Although hailing from South Wales, I spent much of my youth among the brick and tile of the West Midlands, where my parents travelled to find work before my father's early demise. I don't remember my dad and have never seen him since he passed. I realise now that this is not so strange. It is usual for a medium to see little or nothing for their own benefit.

Mum struggled to feed her brood at the expense of what would today be termed 'quality time' with the kids. Life was hard for a single mother with four children in the 1950's. It was not much easier before my dad died. A large chunk of his wages would find it's way into the pub or the bookies before reaching the kitchen table, and on the night I was born, my mother staggered, cold and alone, to the telephone box to call the midwife, while dad drank himself into a stupor down the road.

My childhood world was one of cold lino flooring, hand me down clothes and skipping the free school meals for which I was too proud to queue. Mum was a serious, God fearing woman with a strong Welsh accent, tiny in stature but strict as they come. She was not by nature a demonstrative mother. Ladies of her generation often suppressed their emotions, exchanging them for the strength of character they needed to show if they were to survive.

My teenage sisters, Annette and Helen, were like second mothers to both myself and my big brother Tim, just two years my senior. They helped out all they could as our mum struggled to rear her children on thinned down soup and a prayer. They would step in when she was working, or perhaps asleep after a long night shift, changing our nappies or taking us to school.

One bitterly cold morning Helen took me to the shops in my hand-me-down, squeaky blue pushchair. A woman from the neighbouring street stopped us at the kerb and scolded her without reserve for taking me out without any socks on such a freezing day. My stroppy teenage sister told her to mind her own business, but the remark cut her to the core. It hurt all the more because she knew it was true, but she had no choice. I didn't have any socks. In the weeks that followed Helen saved what pennies she could and one day proudly returned from a trip to Woolworths with a pair of Perlustra socks especially for me – the best in the shop! She was barely more than a child herself, but she doted on her little brothers. When she became a mother many years on, she boasted that babies were nothing new to her. She had done it all before with us.

Although there was no silver spoon for us, no ice creams when the van came around, no bottle of pop to take to the park, when I think back to those days I can appreciate the value of some small acts of kindness from a few big-hearted people.

I could not have been more than three when Helen took me on an errand to pay the coal man who lived a few streets away. Mrs Corkran, his chubby wife, opened the shiny red door, which matched her cheeks perfectly. The terraced house was soot-blackened but the step and doorknocker were immaculate. She and my sister exchanged niceties as I craned my neck to see past her to the bowl of fruit which was displayed on her sideboard, as stately as the crown jewels. I was awestruck. The cut glass sparkled from pride of place on a white lace doily, and the bright colours and simple shapes within it captured my imagination. This lady must be very rich! As Helen said her goodbyes, the generous coal man's wife noticed my wide eyes and open mouth and asked us to wait. She returned a moment later with an orange so huge that I needed two hands to hold it. I ran my tiny fingers over the little bumps on the waxy skin and held it to my nose to inhale the exotic smell. She smiled down at my happy little face and waited for me to thank her.

"What do you say?" Helen prompted

"I've got a brother at home!"

My sister was mortified and apologised through pink cheeks for my bad manners, but Mrs Corkran just laughed and returned to the bowl to fetch another for Tim. I will always remember that walk home, proudly cradling two precious oranges in my jumper.

In my nursery days we had free school milk. A small, tepid bottle with a straw though the cap. For those who had sixpence, there was the added delight of a chocolate covered digestive biscuit in silvery blue foil. The other children would collect their milk and then queue for a biscuit. I never had sixpence so I became accustomed to sitting alone with my drink, gazing at the other children as they licked their chocolatey fingers. One day after everyone was served, the kind teacher lady shouted me to the front.

"There's a biscuit left David. Would you like it?"

My eyes lit up! I still recall how I savoured that biscuit and how for that one day I was like the other kids. I was without doubt the luckiest boy alive. Not until I was an adult did I realise that the teacher must have paid the sixpence herself. I can't remember her name, but God bless her for that. I doubt she realised the little boy would remember her small act of kindness for more than fifty years.

There are some wonderful people in this world. My final Good Samaritan story is about a heroic milkman. It was just before Christmas when Tim and I were still small. My mum was distraught because she had nothing at all to give us. As a single mum, it was hard enough to keep a roof over our heads and food in our bellies. She sat up to the kitchen table and wept. Her boys were excited that Santa was coming, and she was defeated and demoralised. A knock at the door caused her to rise and quickly dry her eyes. It was the milkman to collect his money. He was a down to earth but friendly local chap who spoke with a Birmingham twang. She paid her dues through forced smiles, but as he moved to leave the doorstep the man hesitated. Turning on his heels, he asked her if something was wrong. He must have seen the sadness behind her greeting. She was reluctant and embarrassed to begin with, but after a little pressure she was soon pouring her heart out, relieved for the moment to get her worries out in the open. He was visibly moved by her predicament and encouraged her to dry her tears, explaining it would only upset the family more to see her this way. Having shared her burden, he wished her well and they parted.

Christmas Eve came, and Mum deliberated on what she would say to us in the morning. She went to bed that night with a heavy heart and woke early to light the fire. Opening the front door to lift the milk from the step, she was greeted with a sight that made her cry again, but this time for joy. Next to the pint bottle was a stack of presents wrapped in red Santa paper and addressed to 'The Boys'. There was a cowboy outfit and a tricycle, chocolate and other treats. We had a wonderful Christmas with no idea about our mystery benefactor. In this world of self and greed, it comforts me to realise there is a hidden seam of goodness running through it.

My first recollection of the 'supernatural', although please understand it was nothing if not natural to me, was when I was around five years old.

The night was bitter, and as I huddled under a musty mountain of overcoat blankets, I watched my brother's misty breath flurry and disappear as he slept. Turning to the window my heavy eyes sought out boats and trees and other such little boy's fancies in the icy condensation of the hopscotch panes.

Mum was working. She cleaned hospital floors in the night, to creep up on the germs when they least expected it. Helen had put us to bed, and would look in on us soon. I screwed my eyes up tight and hoped for sleep so that she wouldn't betray me to Mum.

"Boo!"

I caught my breath, startled wide awake as a familiar swish of dark hair in the half-light revealed the identity of my bedtime playmate. I waited, open-eyed now, anticipating the butterflies in my tummy when she did it again. I could hear stifled giggles under the bed.

 Wait for it!

"Boo!"

This time, Mary's shiny, pink face popped up in front of mine. We both laughed, and Tim stirred.

"Shhh!" I hissed, oblivious to the fact it was my laughter that had disturbed him, not hers.

I must have been one of the very few children that looked forward to bedtime. Mary was one of several friends who came to play when I was tucked up and the house was still. She had big brown eyes and lashes like the cows I saw at my granny's cottage in Wales. Her hair was cut short in a thick bob, and I judged her to be around the same age as myself. It didn't occur to my childish mind to ask how she got into my room, or where she hid when we were disturbed. I didn't know that she was dead. I didn't know what 'dead' was. We were friends and the details were irrelevant.

I had other friends like Mary. We played together in my den at the bottom of our council house garden on Eva Road. I had almost forgotten those days. Plimsolled feet striking parched earth, dirty cheeks burning hot, and stinging palms disturbing the cool willow curtain where my companions hid in leafy shadows.

"Can I have a plaster?"

Mum eyed me suspiciously from the washing line. "What for?"

"I hurt my Knee." I lied.

She spat on her hanky and scrubbed the first layer of dirt from the indicated area.

"It's not bleeding. You'll live." A pat on the bum and I was on my way, head hanging.

I just wanted to fit in with my friends. Kevin had a bandage on his head, and Derek wore leg irons. Kevin said he had a brown pony called Chancer, but he never brought it to show me so I wasn't convinced. Helen said ponies weren't for little boys because they cost lots and poo loads. Sally told me how she used to have a really bad tummy ache but then it went. I had decided to pretend that I banged my knee, not wanting to be the odd one out. Sally had long blonde plaits tied with big blue bows. Her gingham dress was always clean no matter how long we played on the dusty floor. Her eyes were the palest blue and her eyebrows almost white. She said I was lucky to see my mum every day. Her grandma took her to see hers sometimes, but when she got there, she didn't think her mum could see her, although her baby brother would sometimes smile in her direction. She just wanted her mother to know that the tummy ache was all better now. She didn't want her to be sad. I told her my mummy got sad sometimes too.

Strange to recall now that I so yearned to be like my spirit friends, when before long I would be trying to ignore them all in a bid to fit in with my peers at school.

Back then there was a comic-book character called Casper. He was a friendly white lump with a wispy tail who floated along and got into all kinds of mischief. I liked the cartoon but made absolutely no correlation between this 'ghost' and the people I saw. I knew they were not quite the same as my mother and my siblings, not so solid, but they were just people and not spooky at all.

When children pass over they are looked after in the spirit world by adoptive guardians, often a relative. Whether they have tragically died young, been miscarried or aborted, they will learn, develop and have a childhood as they would have on Earth if their lives had not been cut short. They play with other children on either side of the veil and from time to time they are brought to visit their parents and family on Earth. So it was with Sally and my other childhood friends.

Children born of any era, any culture are only a breath away from the spirit world they so recently left behind. Like a dream they can't quite remember, their subconscious knows there is something more and is fearless to embrace it. This is why there are so many instances of children seeing family members long gone or having 'imaginary' friends. A new-born baby will look and smile over your shoulder at invisible faces come to say hello. These little ones are as close to pure spirit as you will see in this world. Up to the age of two they are naturally psychic, but between two and five years old it begins to fade. As the years roll on our senses are corrupted by earthly boundaries and expectations, and a mist descends between worlds. Not so with me. I was wired differently somehow, and that veil never fell.

There came a time before too long when the weird things I saw and the strange facts I knew became a source of concern to my family. I was not growing out of it as expected, and they began to worry and wonder what was wrong with me long before I realised that I was different.

One hazy summer afternoon Mum was washing dishes after dinner as Tim and I played with our cars, the linoleum flooring hard beneath our bony knees. A spotlight of sunshine streamed down on us from the window, showing dust in the air from the newly beaten rug.

"When Uncle Bill comes on Sunday can I wear a different shirt?" I asked without looking up. I was wearing one of Tim's cast offs which was still a little big and scratched me at the neck.

Mum turned, drying her hands on her apron. When she didn't reply, I glanced up at her. She was staring at me with a puzzled expression. Tim crashed his car into mine as I turned away and the question was lost to a brotherly scrap and a telling off.

Uncle Bill was a relative I had never met who had not visited with us since I had been born. When Sunday came and so did he, my mother's smiles of welcome were peppered with worried glances in my direction.

"How did you know he was coming?" she asked that night after our Bible story. I couldn't explain. The truth is I didn't know. I hadn't seen or heard anything, I just knew.

As events like this became more common, my mum wasn't sure if it was my sanity or hers she should fear for. The things I said repeatedly came true, and she could no longer ignore my strange behaviour. The last straw came when I ran in from the garden one afternoon that same summer. Washing my hands I asked mum if Aunt Bessie was staying for tea. She was a homely old lady who had been pushing me on the rope swing and telling funny stories. At this Mum suddenly dropped the trifle (incidentally I was devastated at the loss). Apparently this sweet little lady had died many years before I was born.

By the time I was nine or ten the shock which my odd revelations had initially generated was petering out. Mum was still worried, I could sense it, but talk of my latest spirit pal was no longer the talk of the two up, two down Drew house. Helen married and went on to have three children. Motherhood didn't daunt her. As she always said, she had done it all before with me and Tim. After her first little boy she longed for a girl, and despite my advice that she would never have one, bought pink in preparation for each of the next two babies. She had three boys.

When my eldest sister Annette moved away to be a nurse, I proudly occupied the box room she vacated. No more sharing with Tim. I was quite the grown up!

It was in this bedroom one freezing November night that I saw what I thought was an angel. Mum always left the landing light on, and the bedroom door open just a crack so that it shone in, but I loved the dark. There is something of the spirit in the still, velvet blackness. Now that I didn't have to share with my brother I was free to shut the door tight, lie back and just enjoy the peace. I was beginning to relax one night, my icy feet thawing beneath the covers, when a silent flash bathed the tiny room in a golden light. At the centre of the light, just in front of my wardrobe was a beautiful young woman with blonde, shoulder length hair and clothes that twinkled silver. I could look right at her without being dazzled. No wings. Maybe not an angel after all? (The ones on the Christmas cards always had wings). Her face was kind. She smiled at me in silence for some time before she spoke.

"I'm your sister." She paused, then added, "Patricia".

This was a lovely lady, but she was obviously mistaken. Perhaps in the wrong house. I ventured to correct her in my Sunday best voice.

"I am very sorry, but I haven't got a sister called Patricia. I have got two sisters, Helen and Annette and a brother. My name is David."

Her knowing smile widened, and suddenly the room was dark again.

The next morning I dawdled downstairs, following the steam and chatter, to find Tim at the breakfast table, already writing his name in golden syrup on porridge, and mum warming my shirt by the oven. I had just begun my own signature when I remembered my night time visitor. Mum stood behind me, busy at the cooker.

"Last night when I was going to sleep I saw a lady who said she was my sister." I took a mouthful. "She wasn't like the others." I mused. "She looked like an angel. Her name was Patricia."

Tim, who had been disinterested in my story up to now, was suddenly looking over my shoulder, spoon poised, at the back of our mother's head. I turned in my seat. Her shoulders were shaking. What was happening? Surely she wasn't crying? Mum was a strong woman. She had to be.

Life had not been easy for her. The death of her mother found her running the family home, looking after her dad and siblings at the age of fourteen. My father had led her a dance, spending more time and money in the pub than on the family. She was rock solid no matter what, but now I had upset her. I had shaken the unshakable and our foundations were unexpectedly crumbling around us. She took a tea towel from the counter, sank into her chair by the fire and sobbed like her heart would break.

Tears began to well in me too. What had I done? We finished our breakfast in silence. Tim was wide eyed as he passed my balaclava. We shouted awkward goodbyes and began the walk to school. My steps were heavy and my mind elsewhere. I didn't realise how much my seeing people upset Mum. Was she really so worried? Something I said had made her sad. I couldn't bear it. Why was I like this? I decided to turn my back on my spirit friends from now on and be normal. I did try, and for a while I almost succeeded, but ignoring every third person you encounter is not as easy as it sounds, and in the end I couldn't maintain it.

I suppose you would call us latchkey kids. When we let ourselves in that night after school Tim took the task of peeling the potatoes while I consulted the note on the table to receive my directions.

'Peel the potatoes and put them on to boil. Put the sausages in the oven – Gas 5. Will be home around 6. Mam.'

I lit the oven before collaborating with my big brother. I was hoping for some theories as to what was wrong with Mum, but he was as confused as I was by her reaction. I couldn't help but wonder what kind of reception I would get when she got home. Would she still be sad? Angry? Maybe she had forgotten all about it. We decided to lay the table and hope for the latter.

Just after six she came home looking shattered. Throwing off her headscarf and coat, she checked the cooker before calling us to the kitchen table.

"I need to tell you something boys." She spoke slowly without interruption. "Before you were born I had a baby girl. My first born, but she was born dead. They call it 'stillborn'." There was a pause as we took it in. "She was beautiful!" Now the tears came, but this time with some control. I guessed she had probably been crying all day.

"I held her for half an hour before they took her away. We had a little ceremony in the hospital." She looked me square in the eye. "We named her Patricia."

The beautiful lady was my sister after all. She had been telling the truth. Patricia had died as a baby and grown in the spirit world. No wonder she looked so angelic. She never spent a day on Earth. Babies who are still born, miscarried or aborted pass over without committing any sin. When we are born, we all begin with a clean slate. In time, we are presented with worldly situations that stir emotions in us such as jealousy, greed and anger. Life presents us with test after test, but not so for Patricia.

As I grew older, the spirit children appeared less often, but unexpected visitors still took me by surprise from time to time. A hooded monk would periodically appear in the corner by my wardrobe. I never saw the face beneath his hood and he never spoke to me, but he brought an air of serenity so that I soon realised there was nothing to fear. When I woke the next morning I found I had absorbed knowledge from him while I slept. It was quite amazing. Night time in my box room sanctuary became home to the strange and wonderful, and I fell asleep each evening wondering if there would be a mystery guest before morning. When I anticipated them there seldom was, as though they preferred to arrive unannounced.

One such evening whilst sound asleep, I was startled back to consciousness by a loud crack and an explosion of light. It filled the whole room and shimmered from floor to ceiling. Assembling my wits, I dragged into focus an enormous shape at the foot of my bed and for a moment or two I was unsure if I was still dreaming. As the figure spoke my eyes adjusted to the light and my jaw dropped.

"Good Evening," the voice boomed, "I am Blue Cloud."

Is that even a name? I decided not to ask. I have never seen such an imposing man in all my life. Alive or dead here was a man to be reckoned with. His face bore deep furrows and was almost grey in colour. A magnificent feather headdress of coloured light trailed around him, down from the ceiling, past his bare chest and suede trousers, stopping just short of my bedside rug. I peered out from the blankets and as I thought back to cowboy and Indian games, hoped the big chief had come in peace! I could not begin to imagine why such a character would want to visit a ten-year old boy in the West Midlands, but I was not prepared to question such a commanding presence. As he spoke, I realised that this was certainly no dream.

"I am here to help and guide you in your life's work." His arms were folded and his expression stern, but he radiated such a feeling of love that although I felt a little daunted, I was not afraid.

"Thank you," I managed, with absolutely no idea what he meant. "Everyone's asleep!" I hoped he might take the hint and keep his voice down. I was sure the family would hear and burst in at any moment.

He bowed his head. There was an awkward silence, and I felt that since he had taken the trouble to come, I should say something.

"H-Has it been a long time s-since you were on Earth?" I stammered. I wasn't sure of the proper way to word this and tried not to say 'dead' in case he took it as an insult. Here was a person I didn't want to upset! The big man raised his chin, eyes cast down and turned his head to profile. Expanding his chest he drew himself up to what seemed like ten feet.

"I passed in 1647. Age one hundred and twenty-four." His expression remained serious.

I eyed him suspiciously. He looked about sixty to me.

"I have been with you for a very long time – many, many years. I am only ever a thought away."

There was a blast of cold air and the room returned to darkness. He was gone, like a genie disappearing back into the lamp. I lay there for some time, holding my breath, unable to move as I tried to digest what just happened. How could he have known me for many years when I had only been alive for ten? The atmosphere seemed electrified even after he left, like the energy that hangs in the air after a storm. I stared into the blackness, exhilarated and hoping he would reappear until my eyes grew weary and sleep came to take me.

In the months and years that followed Blue Cloud and I became close companions. Despite his commanding presence, when I looked beyond the facade he was warm and sensitive as well as powerful and wise. Only his sense of humour needed work. I found that if I thought about him, he would appear beside me or I would hear him at my shoulder. I discovered I could speak to him telepathically, which avoided the inevitable strange looks from conversing with a Native American chief on the walk to school. He would stand beside me silently as I sat in the park at lunchtime, hungry but too ashamed to queue for the leftovers that were allocated to the kids who had free school meals. I realised then that I never had to be alone. I could call on him any time for help and support. As a schoolboy it seemed to me I had my very own genie.

2
Down to Earth

During the year that followed, Mum decided the appropriate thing to do would be to have me medically checked. Although there was no logical explanation for the things I said coming true, she needed to confirm for her peace of mind that all my screws were intact.

Our first visit to the family doctor in Smethwick was somewhat pointless. She explained to him that I saw and heard things, and we were humoured, fobbed off then shown the door. My mother's Welsh tenacity however, was not to be underestimated. As her anxiety grew, she took me back to Dr Watt time and time again, until at last he agreed to investigate further, and referred me to a child psychiatrist in Birmingham. I could see she was relieved by this, but for my part I was unimpressed. At first I was mildly irritated by the looming appointment. It was a minor nuisance having to catch two buses then hang around for hours on a cold, hard chair surrounded by pot plants. Mum seemed to think it was a positive development and when the day came I was happy to view the situation as a welcome opportunity of an afternoon off school.

My mother was called into the large wooden panelled room first, and the stick thin receptionist assured me that I would not be waiting long. She was wrong. Time crept on and I became increasingly bored, swinging my legs and counting the floor tiles. On the window sill, a starling fluffed up his trembling gullet as he bip-bipped, then warbled to the sleek hen bird who came and went on the ledge. It sounded like he was tuning in Mum's old radio. Eventually, the door opened, and Mum beckoned me in.

Behind a massive mahogany desk sat a tweed-suited, badger-like gentleman peering over half-moon spectacles. He smelled of TCP and Old Spice. His hair was a wispy grey, and his matching goatee swayed as he sucked his tongue. Mum settled me into a leather chair, smiled at us both in turn, then left me to my fate. Somewhere a loud clock ticked and as I waited for him to speak I began to fidget nervously.

"Now then young man! Let's have a chat. Tell me what it is you imagine seeing."

With that one sentence, my opinion of the good doctor was rubber stamped. I realised now for the first time that he suspected I was loopy! Managing to refrain from commenting that one of us certainly was crackers, and it wasn't me, I answered him politely, although with hindsight I am sure my suppressed vexation was evident.

I told him firmly that I didn't 'imagine' seeing anything, and that these people were very real.

He tapped the pen on his chin and mumbled, "I see, I see…"

"No, you don't see. But *I* do!" My response took him by surprise.

His forehead made wavy lines like a toddler's drawing of the sea, then a courteous and heavily disguised interrogation ensued, accompanied by lots of peering, scribbling and a little humming. When at last he had presented me with all his stupid questions, I peeled my legs from the leather seat and called my mother in so that she could hear his conclusion. As the doctor spoke, he leant back in his chair, and I caught a glint from the gold watch chain festooned across his waistcoat. I couldn't help wondering if I was about to be hypnotised. That might be fun.

The reality was less entertaining. It was clear that he was unsure what to make of me. He sieved various unfamiliar words such as 'schizophrenic' and 'psychological' through his beetling moustache, before explaining I would need several consultations if he were to reach a diagnosis.

On the bus journey home I thought about what badger man had said, and for the first time in my life it occurred to me that I might be not only different but abnormal. I certainly didn't conform to what people considered 'the norm'. Might I actually have something mentally wrong with me? I tried to read Mum's face for clues. She was watching the shops drift by through the rainy window with a faraway expression as she fiddled with her gloves. I couldn't read her. I wondered if she was annoyed with me for some reason. She seemed upset or perhaps afraid.

That night as I lay awake, Blue Cloud appeared by the door. I eyed him in silence.

"What do you see?" He asked.

"You." I snapped, puzzled by the question.

"Am I real or imaginary?" He stumbled over the last word but I knew what he meant.

I hesitated. "Real."

"And are you awake or asleep?"

"Awake." I answered.

He gave a nod. "It is good!"

He emphasised these three departing words with clarity and deliberation. In the years to follow he would repeat this phrase many times. My friend had come to reassure me. I turned over and went to sleep.

There were to be two more appointments with the nutty professor. On my last visit, he leant against the bookcase and, observing my eyes drifting to his left, asked me to tell him exactly what I was seeing. A kindly looking lady beside him nodded and smiled as I described her in my childish vocabulary. I waited for the next question, but it didn't come. She spoke softly, a few sentences which I cannot recall but which I relayed to him verbatim. The colour in his face began to fade until it matched his beard. He fell silent, took three shaky steps toward his desk then took a seat, eventually asking me to fetch my mother.

His demeanour seemed different somehow. The air of certainty was gone, and his voice was low. The good doctor ventured that perhaps this was not a medical matter after all. He would not need to see me again.

I thought about his words on the way home, relieved to have been discharged.

"I don't understand it, and quite frankly I don't think I want to."

Putting this short period of self-doubt and concern behind me, I focused in the days ahead on discovering why I was different. There must be a reason for my being this way. I searched for answers where I could, waiting for the one that just felt right. At first, nothing did. I spoke to God daily. Even at this young age I knew He had the answer. I had been weaned on nightly Bible stories and attended Sunday school from the age of eight. When I thought of Jesus, the disciples and apostles it was like coming home. I was sure that God had a purpose for my life. There had to be a reason for this.

In school my R.E. teacher, Mr Spafford recognised in me an enthusiasm for the subject rarely found in a thirteen-year-old boy. He discussed ethics and religion with me, although we did not always agree. He encouraged me to take morning assembly in the school hall, which I did several times, standing proudly on stage in my hand me down uniform. There would be hymns then I would read a passage from the New Testament followed by a short spiritually motivated talk which I had prepared for in class.

I delighted in studying the Bible, reading and re-reading the time honoured stories, and while I accepted the gist, I was sure that the different versions and translations must have been open to a degree of personal interpretation. It was like a beautiful garden that had become overgrown with the weeds of human error. I desperately longed to chop away at those weeds, and then the realisation hit me like a thunderbolt, I felt a calling to become a vicar or priest. I wanted to help people, reassure them about death and teach them about God.

Mother took the news with a raised eyebrow but without rebuke. Her father had been a lay preacher in the Pentecostal Chapel so the idea was not entirely alien, although I doubt she ever expected such designs from either of her rough and tumble sons.

A little research revealed that Christian religions wore many hats, and it became apparent that I needed to find the one that fitted me. I had attended the Baptist Church on Londonderry Lane from the age of twelve, mainly because one had to be a member of the congregation to join the Boy's Brigade, which opened magical portals to such delights as the youth club and five a side football matches. Having already ticked this box I decided to try the Catholic Church next. The building was newly built in brick with a large white cross on the outer wall. I enjoyed several Sunday services there and a few weeks later attended a Methodist Church followed by the Church of England. I was very confused by the similarity. One God, as far as I could tell one Bible, one set of values. What was the purpose of so many different Christian religions? I would sit on the back pew or kneel on the hassock listening to vicars, and from time to time it would be clear to me that their heart wasn't in it. It seemed to me that they were reciting and chanting but not feeling. Once or twice I would just know that the lesson they were preaching was missing the point. I don't know how I knew, and after all, who was I to sit there silently challenging age-old religious teachings? Nonetheless, in my heart I couldn't help it. On the streets of Birmingham I had seen the homeless huddled in doorways, and could not comprehend why the churches didn't open their doors to them. Perhaps they feared their golden candlesticks might be stolen. If so I mused that God would probably prefer them to sell their expensive fixtures, use the money to help these people and thereby eliminate the problem. It made sense to me if no one else.

When members of the congregation chatted at fundraising coffee mornings and the like, they mostly told me that I must believe every word of the Bible. They didn't seem to accept it was written by men who had their personal views and perspectives, or that it had been open to several quite possibly questionable translations. I was puzzled by this. If they actually believed that the Bible in its entirety was the infallible word of God, then why did they shave or cut the hair on the sides of their head, eat pork and shellfish, wear clothes made of more than one cloth and summon the people to prayer with bells? As I read the Bible I discovered all these things were forbidden, yet the people who preached it overlooked this.

In the book of Luke 18:38 it states, 'But the disciples did not understand any of these things. The meaning of the words was hidden from them, and they did not know what Jesus was talking about.' If the people who knew Jesus did not understand, then surely as the word was passed down there is a strong possibility that there could have been mistakes.

There were many other anomalies. Nowhere in the New Testament could I find reference to there being a stable where Jesus was born or any reference to three 'kings'. I still believed in Jesus and the framework of the stories, but would frequently come across something I could not accept. For example; Genesis 3:8 God not being able to find Adam, or Genesis 32, God wrestling with Jacob and pleading for him to let Him go.

Nonetheless, I was happy to accept that there could be another explanation for these strange writings rather than turn my back on the Christian religion with an all or nothing kind of attitude.

It soon became apparent, once I had tested the water, that there was a good chance that religion would be the one to turn its back on me. It seemed that anyone who spoke to the dead was considered to be the spawn of the devil! All of the churches I visited, even though they believed in spirit, did not think that people should communicate with them after death. Since spirit made contact with me whether I liked it or not, I concluded I would quickly be blackballed if I tried to join the clergy. I could never quite grasp the logic that they believed in life after death, but not that you should find out about it. Death is a journey that everyone must make, and as with any journey, it is natural to want to prepare. If they were travelling to a foreign country, I am sure they would first find out about it, what the climate was like, what would be needed there, perhaps even talk to someone who had already been. Why was the subject so taboo? Crestfallen I did try to change their attitude by quoting the scripture. In Mathew 17:1 Jesus is seen talking with Moses and Elijah, who were both long dead, but apparently this is one situation where it is frowned upon to follow His example.

The Nicine Creed begins, 'I believe in one God, the Father Almighty, maker of Heaven and Earth, and of all things visible and invisible.' I could not understand that the Christian faith acknowledges the unseen as being Godly, then condemns in practice what they declare in words.

I realised that there was a further obstacle. If I were a priest I would probably have to abide by precisely what the church wanted me to preach. I had a problem with many of their interpretations so it became obvious I would have to re-think my vocation.

One weekend during the long summer holidays I noticed a turbaned gentleman putting flowers outside a Sikh temple. The fascia reminded me of the wooden building blocks I played with as a boy. Pillars with a triangle balanced on top and semi-circle arches over the doorways.

All that was missing were the bright colours. I paused in thought, and as I did so, the man glanced across at me and smiled. This friendly gesture encouraged me to cross the road and ask if anyone could worship there. I explained that I was not Sikh. He made me welcome and explained a few traditions. Intrigued, I removed my shoes and went inside. The service was pleasant and informative, and the people were very kind. Maybe there were more avenues to explore than I realised.

My horizons broadened, I went the following week to a Synagogue and then a Mosque. I learned that Islam is a peaceful religion, and I am saddened now to think how extreme ideology is poisoning it. I soon realised that each of these religions were well meaning and held a lot of truth, but for me, none had got it just right. People were sorting themselves into boxes labelled by religion, and then fighting each other. I was sure this was not what God intended. Religion is manmade. Men have taken a snippet of truth, manipulated it, adapted it and added an idea or two of their own in order to gain power. But that does not detract from God. It is man who is flawed.

Still I felt a yearning inside. I was frustrated and unsure in my direction. I knew I was here for some reason, and I knew I wanted to help people, but finding the pathway which allowed me to do it was not so easy. I felt sure there was one God and that it didn't matter what you called Him or which road you took to reach Him. If you love Him and love each other, then surely the other teachings take care of themselves? If all religions could open their minds and hearts to each other, I was convinced that the world would take a step in the right direction. A quotation by Rumi summed up just how I felt.

'I looked in Temples, Churches and Mosques, But I found the Divine within my heart.'

We do not go to church to find God. We take Him with us.

Despite my career plans being thwarted, life went on. School work, football, completing my Duke of Edinburgh Award and ignoring the invisible people who tried to get my attention in public places made up my week's itinerary. Mum was more intrigued than worried now regarding what I saw, and she began to open up and tell neighbours and relatives all about it. Some of them were so fascinated that it became commonplace for me to return home from school only to find some stranger sitting in the parlour wanting me to tell them what I saw. When my Auntie Ella visited, she would hand me her empty cup and ask me to read the tea leaves. I would hold it to humour her and just tell her what I saw. Sometimes I would see people in spirit, but not necessarily hear them. At other times, I would hear a voice but not see anyone. New experiences began to evolve as people came to sit before me. The glow that I had always seen around people, not unlike the one on that hot cereal advert, began to change colour and sometimes I would be shown pictures within it as those in spirit tried to convey some message to my guest. I didn't always understand what these pictures meant, but as I experienced them more and more, I began to work out what the signs and symbols represented. A tree branching in two directions was a parting of some kind, the passing of a partner or possibly a divorce, a building that moved was a house move, the offering of a plate represented an opportunity and so on. I also noticed a pattern in the changing colours. Troubled people had a cloudy grey mist; an aggressive person was cloaked in dark red and a considerate, unselfish person in orange.

One ordinary day there was an interesting development. I have learned that very little in this world happens by accident. What my mother described as a chance meeting at a bus stop one November afternoon, with hindsight was quite obviously no coincidence.

She was standing in the shelter one Friday afternoon on the way to collect her wages from the Town Hall, when an elderly lady, who at five feet two inches was still considerably taller than she was, engaged her in conversation. As they chatted, the woman's warm and engaging demeanour encouraged my mum to open up about her concerns regarding her youngest son and his strange visions. The lady lit up, explaining that she understood all about this kind of thing and she introduced herself as Nelly Woolley, President of Smethwick Spiritualist Church. She offered to help, assuring my mother that there was nothing to worry about. That evening mum came home with a spring in her step and an appointment for us to meet with this fascinating lady the following Tuesday after school.

Jumping down from the bus that evening, I caught up with my mum who was consulting a scrap of paper as she walked. Her heels clip-clopped on the uneven paving slabs and came to rest outside the tiny terraced house. Mum looked me up and down and once satisfied with my appearance she straightened her hat and knocked twice on the bright blue door. A slight lady with silver hair, fair skin and blue rimmed glasses welcomed us in. I followed the women, wondering how much grown up talk I would be made to endure. The house was larger than it appeared from the outside. We entered the hall, passing an immaculately kept lounge on the left before entering the cosy living room situated at the end of a shadowy corridor. A kettle rattled on the kitchen stove beyond, and I settled into a faded wing back chair to await biscuits and the approaching chink of china cups on melamine tray.

Mrs Woolley perched on the floral patterned chair opposite mine and as the nattering commenced my eyes wandered to the heavy red drapes, alabaster figurines and wall full of old books. I breathed in their fusty smell and wondered if she had read them all. The atmosphere was warm and friendly. As the adults spoke, I began to sense spirit all around us. I felt comfortable and safe.

Suddenly she turned from my mother and smiled directly at me.

"I can see a giant of a man behind you David. He is dressed like a North American Indian."

I froze, cup in hand. My eyes must have been as large as the saucer I held, but I couldn't speak. Now she had my attention.

"His name is...... something Blue."

I swallowed the tea. "Blue Cloud," I said.

"Yes! That's him." She leant forward and smiled. "He's your spirit guide, and he will always be with you."

I had never met a living soul who could see what I saw, and had come to believe, in my naivety, that I never would.

I listened awestruck as she went on to explain that she had seen spirit all of her life, then she asked me if I saw anyone with her. Thus began an exciting ping pong match of who saw what with who, going back and forth between us until I noticed my mother's expression. Her eyes were glossy with a mixture of relief and amazement. She must have felt very out of place. There was no history of psychics in our family, no hint of anyone else with these gifts, so this was very much unchartered territory for her. In this house, she was the odd one out, and I knew that feeling well. I had found someone else who could see and hear the things I did, and more importantly, I felt reassured that she had verified my sanity.

This day marked the beginning of a very unlikely friendship between a fourteen-year-old boy and a seventy-five-year-old woman. Mrs Woolley was an inspirational lady and over the years that followed, I came to love her dearly. I called at her house most days after school, and we talked for hours. She would have a cup of tea, an ashtray and a strawberry flan waiting for me, and I would sit enthralled as she explained the names of the psychic gifts, and how they could be a blessing or a curse.

She told me that we each have a spirit guide who is with us whenever needed, but steps behind a curtain in more private moments. In addition we have many helpers who may come and go as required.

I was unfamiliar with the word 'psychic' and was relieved when she told me that it only meant that I was perceptive concerning spiritual influences. All natural mediums are very sensitive by nature. When I saw people in spirit, it was apparently called clairvoyance, meaning 'clear seeing'. What is more, there are two types of clairvoyance, objective when I saw spirit with my eyes, and subjective where people may see pictures in their head.

When I heard them speak to me, it was called clairaudience. Mrs Woolley told me how many mediums were only clairsentient, meaning they neither see nor hear, but merely sense the spirit world.

I learned that the glow I saw around people was called the Aura. It is the life force of all living things, which is the reason I also see it around animals and growing plants, and why it fades from the flower in the vase as it dies. In humans, it is considered the clothing of the spirit. When we die, it deserts the corpse and goes with our spirit to the next world. There are many layers to the aura, rather like a rainbow, and it can stretch outwards from the body for up to three feet or even further, although clarity does diminish towards the edge. By studying the aura, which is constantly changing with mood and circumstances, one can learn about a person's emotions, personality, the conditions around them and any health problems they may have. Mrs Woolley explained to me that although most people do not see the aura, many are aware of it. They will instinctively know for example when someone is standing behind them as they feel their auras touch.

In the playground I tried it with my 'normal' friends. They held out their arms, with hands about two feet apart, then they slowly moved their palms together. When they were still inches away, the boys reported feeling a force, like repelling magnets, which grew stronger as their hands moved closer together. I explained that they were feeling the aura. In another playground game, a selected child faces the wall and tries to catch playmates who sneak up behind them. You can feel when someone is behind you, auras touching, without seeing or hearing anything. You may have noticed this yourself when standing in queues.

On the advice of my new mentor, I attend my first Sunday service at the Spiritualist Church on Thimblemill Road in Smethwick. Despite all my searching I had never heard of this religion, so I set about learning what I could. Spiritualism has its roots in the belief in survival after death. There are various spiritualist groups around the world which differ in the detail of their faith. In 1848 in Hydesville New York, modern spiritualism was born when the Fox sisters first documented spirit communication in the form of knockings in their house. The girls would ask questions and were answered in a code of raps. In 1862 President Lincoln visited medium Nettie Maynard, whose guide told him that war would not end until slavery was abolished. It was just days afterwards that he declared all slaves in the United States were to be set free. Our own Queen Victoria frequently visited a medium after the death of her husband, and Prime Minister William Gladstone was quoted as saying. 'Psychic research is the most important work which is being done in the world today.'

By the 1870s, many spiritualist groups were calling themselves churches. The movement began to grow, reaching a peak between the world wars. In 1931 The Greater World Christian Spiritualist League was formed with the aim of uniting churches and individuals. They were inspired by Christian teachings but added the truth of survival after death.

Like any other place of worship, the reason to attend a Spiritualist Church should be to praise God. If you receive a message from a loved one, that is a bonus, but it should not be the reason for your visit.

The brick built building on Thimblemill Road had been sold to Spiritualists by the Catholic Church when they moved to their lovely new location. Although they utterly abhorred the practice of contacting the spirit world, it seems they were not averse to selling their church to Spiritualists, whose meetings were historically hidden in back rooms for fear of reproach. No group of people have been more misunderstood than mediums. At one time they were worshipped, then they were burned as witches. In modern days, they figure as mystics or cranks. Little wonder then that many psychics hide their experiences from the world rather than be laughed at or condemned. Modern spiritualism was now out of the closet however, and the Smethwick church was fantastic. The heart of a church is not bricks and mortar but the harmony created by the people who meet there to pray, however it was nice somehow to be able to meet in a purpose-built church.

I ventured inside and sat on the back row, trying to be inconspicuous. Around fifty people sat in the pews which stretched out before me to the rostrum, where Mrs Woolley sat next to an elderly lady which the posters named as 'Sally Fergusson'. The atmosphere was pleasant and sociable. After a couple of hymns, Mrs Fergusson was introduced as the guest medium and slowly stood up to speak. She was a wiry lady with grey hair and a cheerful disposition. After giving a short talk on the fatherhood of God and the brotherhood of man she began to point to members of the congregation, telling them who was with them in the spirit world and what advice they had to offer. Here was a place where a person who sees dead people was not only accepted but welcomed. As I pondered on this, thinking myself safely hidden in the crowd, I heard these words,

"I want to come to the young man at the back."

Everyone turned to look at my crimson face. I felt exposed.

"You are very psychic my dear, and one day you will be doing what I am doing now. I can see from the colours in your aura, purple, blue and green that you should be healing."

With that, she moved on, and I was left to recover my composure. In theory I knew that I was capable of passing messages on, but could not in a million years envisage myself doing it in front of such a huge crowd of people. As for healing, I was confused as to what this meant so I asked Mrs. Woolley about it the following day after school.

Spiritual Healing is a very real power. It is a sacred gift that is as old as the world itself. It is not to be confused with faith healing which implies that faith is required, as babies, animals and people who do not believe are also cured. The healing energy comes from God and is channelled through angels, then those in the spirit world, (often doctors), and it is then administered through the healer's hands, the last link in the chain. The healer is a passive instrument. The benefits are genuine and results vary from pain relief to a complete and lasting cure. The underlying principle of spiritual healing is that we are all intended to live our lives in good health until it is time to pass over. Any deviation from perfect health is contrary to nature's intent. Illness is a state of imbalance which needs to be corrected, whether it be physical, emotional or mental. She explained that the healer should never promise a cure, but offer it up to God and yield to His will, then she stressed that we must never discourage anyone from seeing their doctor. Spiritual healers should work hand in hand with the medical profession, not in competition with it.

Mrs Woolley invited me to sit in her circle where I could meet with a dozen or so like-minded people and develop my healing ability. They met every Friday night at her home to hold what you might call a séance. She explained that all circles are simply psychic experiments, and the results are not guaranteed. Sitters would share their experiences and develop their own psychic gifts. She described me as a natural medium and said she was sure that despite my age (it was usually unheard of for a minor to sit) I would be at home with the experience, and it would be of benefit to me.

Friday came, and as I entered the house which was by now a home from home, it was apparent that I was the last to arrive. Every chair and standing space in the living room was occupied, and ten unfamiliar smiles welcomed me like an old friend. They were evidently expecting me. There were only two men, and all the sitters were aged between fifty and eighty. Mrs Woolley introduced me to the group as they sipped their tea, but I was too overawed for the names to stick. One lady, Mrs Delaney reminded me of Ena Sharples of 'Coronation Street' fame, complete with hairnet and dowdy full length overcoat, which she seemed reluctant to remove.

Everyone exchanged mundane chit-chat until the mantle clock struck seven and the group arranged their chairs into a circle. There were bentwood dining chairs, wing back arm chairs and a couple of stools brought in from the kitchen. I sat next to Mrs Woolley, who told me to relax and breathe deeply. The man in a blue pullover lit the candle on the small mahogany table in the centre of the group, and a lady called Margaret simultaneously reached to switch off the lights. Mrs Woolley began with a prayer, asking for guidance and protection. Some soft instrumental music played in the background and as I began to unwind a cold breeze rippled around my feet, despite the fact that my face was burning hot. Temperature anomalies were apparently a common occurrence within the circle.

The candle flickered, throwing giant dancing shadows on the walls, and as my eyes relaxed into the monochrome surroundings, I began to see spirit all around. The shapes of relatives and friends faded in around the other sitters, but there were other characters who seemed more out of place. These multi-cultural and old fashioned people were the guides and helpers of the group members. One of the gentlemen whispered that he could see a small clown beside me with a bowler hat and a big flower. Mrs Woolley explained that this was a spirit helper of mine. We have one guide who stays with us from birth she told me, and several helpers who may come and go as required. I looked to my left and was perplexed that I couldn't see him. I learned that there are many different dimensions, like channels on a radio, and it depends on which wavelength you are tuned in to as to who you can see. Stranger still, you may see two people in spirit who are from different dimensions and can therefore not see each other. The spirit world was not as straightforward as I had assumed.

After the closing prayer, the lights were switched on, and the candle extinguished with a wish. Everyone took a moment to come back to earth before restoring the room to its former glory. I had never felt so peaceful, relaxed and invigorated all at the same time, as though I had experienced a kind of spiritual shower.

It was not long before the little clown made himself known to me in person. He began to crop up in the most unlikely situations, often making me laugh at the most inconvenient moment. I noticed that he tended to appear when I was stressed or feeling down. He had an incredibly infectious laugh, and I soon found myself developing an unexpected affection for my little helper. His clothes reminded me of Charlie Chaplain but his face was painted white, and he wore the traditional red nose. In quieter moments when he stopped playing the fool, he told me that his name was Pepe and that he came from Italy. When I asked how he passed to spirit, he looked sad, and I saw for the first time a glimpse of the real man. In softer tones he explained that an acrobat had fallen from the trapeze during the circus performance and the clowns were sent in to distract the distressed crowd. Children were crying as she was carried off and Pepe was desperate to cheer them up. He climbed up to the high wire, fooling around all the time. He had walked the tightrope many times, but before reaching the safety of the platform, his foot slipped and he fell to his death before the eyes of the audience. His remorse was visible even after all these years.

"It was my job to cheer people up. Sometimes there were mums, dads and kids and I had to make them all laugh. I had to make them happy. The dads were always the ones – they sat with long faces. Mums were OK, and it was easy to make the kids laugh, but it wasn't easy to make the dads happy. You know how I made the dads happy? I made the kids happy first. If the son is happy the father is happy."

He confessed sadly that he made everyone unhappy that day. He wanted to make them laugh, but instead he made them cry.

Each Friday I returned to the circle, learning and experiencing new things in the company of people who thought like I did. Some of them had been patiently sitting for years even though they hardly saw anything themselves. Their dedication was not lost on me.

On one occasion, just before the circle, Mrs Delaney remarked that she had a headache, and I was encouraged by Mrs Woolley to place my hands on her head and 'tune in', as she put it, to the spirit world. In the instant she sat before me, a nauseating stabbing pain struck my temples. As I stood and prayed, I was aware of a Chinese man building up to my left. His demeanour suggested a placid and unassuming soul. He wore a traditional, conical hat and beneath his gentle smile dangled a thin grey beard. Words came softly as he explained he was here to help me with the healing, and would remain with me for as long as he was needed. He added I should call him Yeung.

Mrs Delaney was the first to tell me she felt a force, a warmth and vibration coming from my hands as the headache melted away.

From time to time, Tim would ask if he could accompany me to circle. He and I spent most of our free time playing football or wrestling in the house, to the despair of our mother and the detriment of the china cabinet we smashed. He was intrigued by my new pastime and wanted to share in it. Mrs Woolley kindly welcomed him, but he would sit like a statue, gripping my hand and sweating profusely, unable to relax at all. Afterwards, Margaret would offer us a lift home with her husband in their Reliant Robin. Tim would spend the journey vowing never to go back, but a few weeks later, like a moth to the flame, he would develop the urge to repeat the performance all over again. To this day, he is torn between fear and a fascination for the afterlife and the unusual abilities of his little brother.

After suffering a nasty knee injury while playing football one winter, Tim was told that he needed an operation. There was a lengthy waiting list and as time went on the pain began to wear him down. I decided to see if I could help. Knowing he would be far too nervous to receive contact healing, I decided to administer absent healing, which I had learned about in the Spiritualist Church. With the power of thought, which is a very real force, healing is directed to the person in need. Spirit doctors can travel in an instant to the patient's side, no-matter where in the world they are. This would be the perfect way to ease Tim's pain without frightening him, so one evening while he was in bed I meditated, directing my thoughts and prayers towards his injured knee before falling asleep. The next morning, far from being oblivious to the healing he had received, Tim was bursting to tell me about the terrifying experience he had during the night. My plan not to alarm him had apparently failed. He had felt himself lifting out of his body, hanging suspended above the bed while invisible hands manipulated his knee. I had to confess what I had done and explained that many people are not even aware of it when they receive absent healing. Forgiveness for the experience didn't come until he realised his pain had almost gone, and the doctors told him he no longer needed an operation.

One Friday evening after a particularly tiring day, I was so exhausted that I almost didn't go to circle. I toyed with the idea of an early night but at the last minute decided to make the effort. As I relaxed under the protection of the circle, my eyes began to feel heavy. Suddenly my chin dropped to my chest, and I jolted awake, heart pounding and mortified to realise that I had fallen asleep! The other circle members were staring at me. My cheeks reddened, and I began to mutter an apology, but Mrs Woolley held up her hand to stop me. She told me I had been in trance for around twenty minutes. I felt bewildered as she explained that a little girl called Rose had been using my body to speak and apparently made everyone laugh as I squirmed around on my chair. At first, I could not process this information. I was disorientated and confused, not fully understanding what had happened.

When the evening was over, and all the sitters had gone, I stayed with Mrs Woolley for a while. I was trembling inside and felt shaken and somehow out of sync with the world. We sipped sweet tea from willow patterned cups as she explained what had happened. With trance mediumship, physical phenomenon is experienced. There are varying levels of trance, and it seems I had been in deep trance and was therefore totally unaware of what was occurring. The spirit (or soul) is joined to the body by a cord which shines with a silvery light. Mine had left my body, still attached by this silver cord, and had been held in a hypnotic type state. Whilst in what I took to be a natural sleep, the spirit of Rose entered my body to communicate directly with the group. She described it as slipping a hand into a glove. I learned that the degree of control the person has over the body is variable. Some may only be able to speak whilst others have full and accurate control over the body, which is achieved by the use of psychic energy, usually drawn from the other sitters like a battery. In some instances, this energy can be used to build the facial features of the person in spirit rather than to speak. This phenomenon is called transfiguration. She stressed what a rare and precious gift this is, and although she was a trance medium herself I was surprised to learn that there are only a handful in the world.

As we parted, Mrs Wooley put her arm around my shoulder and softly told me that trance mediumship opens a door to new fields of knowledge and experience and that I should not be afraid. My guide, Blue Cloud would decide who to allow to come through, and I would be perfectly safe. She told me that spirit control can stimulate unused areas of the brain and improve psychic development.

As a regular sitter in Mrs Woolley's circle, many people came to speak through me in trance or showed themselves by means of transfiguration. As spirit honed me as an instrument, they were eventually able to slip in and out with ease, although afterwards I was always left exhausted and disorientated. My guides and helpers regularly spoke to the group, and Rose, who in life had spina bifida, became a frequent visitor to the circle. Several other personalities would often speak through me, at the discretion of Blue Cloud, who acted as my doorkeeper. He would stand between worlds, only allowing those he deemed appropriate to occupy my body, and ensuring they didn't stay too long. One character was a young man who would make an appearance from time to time in a highly distressed state. He would weep and cry out, unable to answer the circle members when they asked him questions. Weeks went by before he eventually offered his name as Tim. When the sitters asked what was wrong, he just said he didn't understand, and it wasn't fair. After several months, he became calmer and began to open up a little more, until at last one of the older members of the group realised who he was. His name was Timothy Evans, a Welshman who had been wrongfully hanged for the murder of his wife and baby daughter in 1950. His neighbour John Christie had strangled them and hidden their bodies in an outhouse. The murderer concealed his guilt by offering incriminating testimony at Timothy Evans' trial. Three years after Evans' execution, Christie was exposed as a serial killer when more bodies were found at his property. He had been free to murder six other women, including his wife, as a result of this miscarriage of justice. No wonder Timothy was so distraught. He had passed to spirit in the most horrific and unjust way.

When people sit in circle their guides stand behind them, creating a protective ring of highly spiritual beings. The circle itself then emits a light, which shines like a beacon throughout the spirit world. There are certain circumstances under which people pass to spirit and find themselves lost for a while in a very dark and lonely place. This may be because they have committed suicide and are very confused, or perhaps they had no belief in an afterlife and cannot comprehend that they still exist. They may find themselves in a dark environment with no physical body, and it often takes some time for them to realise that the fact that they are thinking means that they must, in some form, still be alive. In the case of Timothy Evans, his turmoil was due to his life being prematurely snatched away, leaving him feeling cheated and confused. If you were lost in the night in the middle of nowhere and you saw a light in the distance you would quite naturally gravitate toward it. Rescue circles are formed with the sole purpose of benefiting those who have died and lost their way. These people are attracted by the light and come to the circle, where people are waiting to assist them reach their destination. So it was with Timothy Evans. He felt the need to make contact with the earth and get his story and all his emotions out. Speaking to the sitters helped him come to terms with the reality of what had happened, and then he was ready to be rescued by those in spirit. Blue Cloud and the other guides were able to assist him in crossing over to where he was supposed to be, a place where he could learn and progress. His visits to our circle then came to an end, and we did not hear from him again until around two years later, when he came back to thank us all for our help.

It was not too long before Mrs Fergusson's prediction came true and I was coaxed into taking my place on the rostrum of the Spiritualist Church. Mum was incredibly excited. She made a special visit to the hairdressers and even bought a new hat to be sure she looked her best for the Sunday evening service. (She considered it sacrilege to be seen in church without a hat!)

As the hour approached, I began to regret my decision. My juddering nerves were only steadied by the confidence that my friends in spirit would be there for me. As I entered the church with my mother on my arm, I stopped short at the door and caught my breath. The pews were crammed, well over a hundred people had come to see me. I was not prepared for this. I had never seen such a sizeable crowd there. Mum chose a seat at the back of the room as I took my place on the rostrum, heart pounding.

As the congregation warbled the last refrain of the first hymn, I rose to my feet. The room was spinning and my legs wavered beneath me, but I gathered my senses and put one metaphorical foot firmly in the spirit world as I was introduced as the youngest medium to take a service. Here we go!

The congregation settled into their seats, and I breathed deeply, waiting for a sign. The room hushed and time seemed to slow. Come on! The silence was tangible.

Then I saw her. A girl of around twelve was standing in the aisle next to a nervous looking couple. Someone whispered "Sarah" in my ear, and I knew it would be ok. Around the room, a scattering of new arrivals formed beside their seated loved ones. An old man with a cap rested his hand gently on one lady's shoulder, and there was even a small white dog running along the front row.

I relayed what I was seeing to the people concerned. I refused to be one of those mediums who say, "Does anyone know a George." If I couldn't be more specific, I moved on to the next message. I noticed that when someone in the congregation spoke back to me, the link seemed to strengthen. A 'hello' from the right person was all that I needed to make the message clearer. Quietly at first, but then with more confidence, I lost myself in the stories of strangers. Suddenly it seemed my allocated time was up, and I took my seat next to Mrs Wooley, who announced the final hymn. When I stepped back into this world, I was a little dazed but also extremely exhilarated. I swelled with the most satisfying sense of achievement and at last I could see a possible explanation of why I was born this way. Tearful parents, husbands and daughters gathered around me as the room began to empty. They had been comforted by the things I told them and they lingered to thank me one by one, some hoping to hear one last word from their loved one. Smiling through their tears, it seemed as though a weight had been lifted from them.

Things began to slot into place. This must surely be my purpose. I had not considered that talking to those in the spirit world could help anyone, after all, I could not bring anyone back, yet these people seemed content just to have some personal confirmation that their loved ones were living on somewhere.

Exhausted now my eyes sought out my mother. Her seat was empty, and I was tired and eager to make headway homeward. A crowd gathered at the door as they filed out onto the street and there was Mum, peacock proud at the entrance, greeting everyone as they left with the words, "That's my son! That was my son." All the years of worry and stress I had put her through welled in my eyes. My mum was proud of me. All was well with the world.

School, circle, football, church was perhaps not a typical adolescence. Only a few of my closest friends knew of my strange lifestyle. When playing in the football team I would glance up to see Pepe running along the side-line, his little arms and legs flailing to make me laugh. Despite such occurrences, I tried to live an otherwise normal life, with the consolation now that at least I knew I was not the only one with a foot in each world.

I was by no means squeaky clean, however. When I was fifteen, there was an incident in my geography class which resulted in my being expelled. The class was arranged in double rows of wooden, ink-welled desks, and my class mate Kevin sat to my left by the window. Our teacher, Mr Wilson, commonly known as 'Popeye' by his students, was droning away, erasing the last assignment from the board as he spoke through a fog of chalk dust. Turning to the class, he spotted Kevin on the front row, staring through the window in a world all his own. White mist turned to red, and Popeye lunged toward Kevin before either of us could react. He leant over me, textbook flapping, and proceeded to clout him repeatedly about the head. I ducked down but was unable to dodge the occasional incidental blow. I admit I was irritated.

"Hey, hey!" I stood up to step out of my seat. "If you are going to hit him at least let me get out of the way!"

"You have one too Drew, for your cheek!"

The thick volume landed hard on my ear.

Without stopping to think I grabbed him by the lapels and pinned him up against the blackboard, fist poised. I could taste the chalk in the air as I stared into his startled face and just about managed to stop myself from making the blow. My school days were over.

That night there was no visit from Blue Cloud, although I could feel spirit all around me. I had behaved badly. I knew I had let them down, and I was ashamed.

The next day I began to look for work. I had held a paper round for two years, which funded my secret smoking habit, but now I found myself in a position to bring a much-needed wage into the home. That Saturday afternoon on a shopping errand to nearby Bearwood, I noticed a sign in George Mason's grocery store which indicated they were in need of staff. I went inside and expressed my interest to the serious gentleman stacking tins inside, hoping to perhaps be invited for an interview. He was tall and immaculately dressed, with glasses and a tuft of dark hair over each ear. He introduced himself as shop manager Sid Whittington, and to my surprise he gave me the job there and then. I left school that week and entered the world of work.

I was deployed to the provisions counter slicing bacon, cheese and cooked meats. My impressive weekly wage was five pounds and ten shillings, which I was proud to turn over to my mum. She duly returned one pound ten shillings to me for bus fares and lunch money.

I was happy in my work and spirit friends would pop up in the shop from time to time. Rose began to show herself to me while I was working and would rejoice in playing little tricks like poking her finger into the butter. Mr Whittington was a kindly gentleman who I soon came to look up to and respect.

One Saturday afternoon I was busy slicing ham for a lady, when I glanced up to see Mrs Woolley looking in through the shop window. She smiled hello and came inside. When I next looked up from my task, I was puzzled to see her deep in conversation with Mr Whittington. They were laughing and joking like old friends. When I was free she seized the opportunity and came across for a quick chat.

It appeared that Sid Whittington was treasurer of the Spiritualist Church and a spiritual healer himself. We had each been keeping our unusual gifts to ourselves, unaware that we had shared interests.

When I look back at this period in my life, there were far too many coincidences. Mum meeting Mrs Woolley and my applying for a job with Mr Whittington were obviously opportunities presented by those in spirit to help me understand my gifts and ultimately use them to help people. Our guides and helpers put the wheels in motion every day, trying to steer us in the right direction. Unfortunately, the devil's workers do the same in an attempt to throw us off course. The trick is to recognise which is which - not always as easy as you might think.

3
Death and Destruction

As a young adult, I began to embrace with some enthusiasm the exciting world of alcohol and girls. I almost resented the interference of Blue Cloud and others in spirit, who seemed to take up far too much of my time. It was my life after all. Often I would make a point of ignoring them in a futile effort to rebel. I enjoyed going out for a few drinks with my friends, and I am ashamed to say that in my naivety I used my psychic abilities on more than one occasion to impress the ladies with a party trick or two, identifying playing cards or selecting which coin they had touched.

One Thursday evening when I was nineteen, I went with a small group of friends for our weekly night out in Birmingham. It was an evening that I would not forget. We began in The Mulberry Bush, a well frequented pub in the city centre where we had one pint and a cigarette or two before moving on. Our next stop was The Tavern in the Town, situated in the famous Rotunda building just a few yards further down New Street. We walked into the smoky bar and ordered a beer, laughing and joking as we argued about the next potential hostelry on our epic pub crawl. From the Juke box, local band made good 'Slade' played 'Merry Christmas Everybody', somewhat prematurely maybe, but the mood was festive despite there being a whole month to wait until the season hit.

The sound we heard next, I will never forget. The pub walls trembled, lights dipped, and the ground beneath us shook as a colossal explosion moved the very air around us. Disbelief then dread swept through every nerve of my body as we all instinctively ran outside into the beating rain.

The Mulberry Bush had gone. Rubble and toxic smoke filled the street, along with a weird, putrid smell. Alarms set off by the blast were sounding all around. Hundreds of people ran aimlessly about, bleeding from the flying glass and desperately calling out for loved ones. We stood in shock as splinters and dust rained onto our hair and shoulders. The smoke began to disperse, and I noticed what I thought was a bundle of smouldering rags in the gutter. As the image cleared, I could see it was a severed arm adrift in a sea of blood and rain. Here and there shoes, ripped clothing and more body parts just lay in the road. Sick to the stomach, we realised that the strange smell was burning flesh. One of the lads said that we should make our way home. Our parents would be worried. In a world without mobile phones there was no obvious way to put their minds at rest. Quickening our steps we found ourselves running away from the chaos. Ambulances and police cars screamed all around and then - a second explosion behind us stopped us in our tracks. The Tavern in the Town, where just ten minutes ago we had left our drinks, had been destroyed by another IRA bomb. We headed out of the city. Twice in one evening we had evaded death. Twenty-one others had not been so lucky.

Setting off on foot we joined the tide of people heading down Hagley Road. Bus services had been cancelled. We tried to hail a taxi, but every one sailed past us. Later we discovered they were picking up the injured as there were not enough ambulances to deal with the carnage. Unbeknown to us, a third bomb failed to explode outside one of the banks we passed on the journey home. Once more we had miraculously escaped without injury. In addition to the dead, 182 people were badly hurt that night, and the lives of many others changed forever.

That night lying safe in my bed, it took some time for me to fall asleep. The horrors of the evening were spinning in my brain. When at last I closed my eyes the ceiling seemed to part, revealing a cloudy sky and a burst of shooting stars falling to Earth. As the scene became clearer, I realised I was not seeing stars, but spiritual beings rushing down to scoop poor confused victims up to safety.

The newly deceased were in shock and could not fully grasp what had happened, but rescue parties from worlds beyond were working hard to help them. It was a sad and yet beautiful sight. My heart sank as I thought of the families who had lost someone that night, for whom there would be no comfort.

The act of dying is in itself nothing to fear. It is as simple as passing from one room to the next. Of course, we all hope for the prelude to death to be pain-free, but the real pain is borne by the loved ones who grieve for our presence beside them long after our trauma has ended.

There are many ways to die. Someone who has passed in hospital after a chronic illness may find themselves transported to very familiar surroundings. Spirit hospitals exist not to heal the body, but to aid in the emotional recovery of those who need time to adjust to their new situation and the reality they are now free from physical illness. Those who passed in the tragedy of that night may not have realised at first what had happened. Each man's death is his own story, but often people who die as the result of an accident do not initially realise they are dead. They may stand up, thinking they have had a miraculous escape and wonder why those around don't interact with them. The high spirit beings I saw that night were sent to rescue people such as these who were confused or lost. There was help for them that night.

When we die, we do not become spirit. We are spirit before we die. The earth is just one plane of existence among many, the only dimension in which our spirit needs a vehicle, which it finds in the form of a body. When death comes, we throw off this cumbersome suit with all its problems and limitations, and we soar! We may be greeted by old friends and lost relatives, who come to help us adjust to our new existence. I am reminded of the arrivals lounge at the airport, where faces light up as souls are reunited. The next step comes when your spirit guide and helpers analyse with you every event in your earthly life - your actions, your thoughts, your words and more importantly how they affected others. There is no language barrier here because there is no speech as we know it. Communication is made by means of thought transference or telepathy. After this has been accomplished your new home is revealed to you. You will go to a plane of existence where everyone is at the same stage of spiritual development as yourself, and here you will continue to learn.

My personal first-hand experience of losing a loved one came sooner than I ever imagined it would. Mum had suffered from headaches for as long as I could remember.

Painkillers were essential items on the shopping list every week as common as the bread and milk.

I was twenty-four and living in a house around the corner from home when I noticed that she was getting worse. Every Saturday I would drive her into town to have lunch in an old fashioned café as my treat. Sometimes someone in spirit would be standing behind the person at the next table, pleading with their eyes for me to tell their loved one they were there. I had to look away. Once in George Mason's I had been naïve enough to tell a lady that her husband was with her, and it did not go at all well. She was startled and reacted badly. I learned at that moment not to pass on a message from spirit unless invited to do so. In the café, I kept my eyes on my tea cup and made small talk with Mum. She told me how the doctor had diagnosed migraine and given her something stronger for the pain. The family had noticed she was becoming uncharacteristically tearful and very forgetful. It was obvious she was getting worse, but that said, none of us suspected anything sinister. I took her out on day trips to cheer her up. We visited the coal mining village of Cwmaman where she grew up, and she sat on the swing where she played as a child. Another time I took her to Gretna Green, where strains of a lone piper playing Amazing Grace moved her to tears.

At last, the doctor elected to dig deeper and carry out some routine memory tests, a series of straightforward questions designed to identify if there was any cause for concern. First, she was asked the name of the Prime Minister, then what day of the week it was. She became so frustrated when she couldn't answer either question. "Of course I know," she said, "it's on the tip of my tongue!" He referred her to a neurologist, and her appointment came through quicker than we expected. She would have to be an in-patient for a couple of days while they conducted various tests. She was not happy about the idea. With no smoking in the hospital, two days promised to be a very long time. We encouraged her with the promise that the problem would be sorted out at last.

It was on the second day that Tim and I went together to visit her. I have always hated hospitals. If I am in the presence of someone who has a headache or a backache, I feel their condition, so these places are not pleasant for me. The smell of disinfectant as we walked down the pastel green corridors was making my stomach flip. We followed the directions to the ward as laid out by our sisters, then asked at the nurse's station for Mrs Drew's bed. The Sister picked up a cream coloured phone and appeared to be notifying someone of our arrival. We exchanged anxious glances as a doctor emerged from the office opposite and ushered us inside as he introduced himself. Tim's colour dissipated into a kind of ash grey.

The specialist talked without hesitation as he slotted two x-rays onto the lighted wall, but his words seemed to come in slow motion, taking a moment or two to reach my brain before I could process the meaning.

"I need to talk to you about your mum. Look at this." He indicated a shaded area on the x-ray. "This is a tumour embedded deep in her brain. I can operate to remove it but to do so, I would have to take with it a vital section of the brain. The location means that your mum would probably lose all cognitive function. I'm so sorry, but I need to ask you what you want me to do."

The words came like a blow to the stomach that took away my breath. Tim spoke first. "What happens if you don't operate?"

"She won't last more than six months. I'm sorry. It's a tough decision to make."

There was a helplessness in my older brother's eyes as he searched my face for an answer. It was my turn to speak now.

"Let her go."

The doctor addressed Tim. "Do you need some time to decide?"

He shook his head. "Whatever David says."

Once back in the room, it took us a minute or two to regain our composure. We couldn't let mum see us in this state so we regrouped and painted on a positive attitude as best we could. We agreed not to tell her.

As we entered the room, she was sleeping, or so we thought. We kept our voices low so as not to disturb her; then Tim noticed she was pursing her lips.

"She wants to kiss you!" he said.

I shot him a look that told him he was stupid. She was a strong woman, a survivor but she had never been demonstrative. I don't ever remember her hugging or kissing me, and I couldn't see her starting now.

"She wants a fag!" I lit a cigarette, put it to her lips and she inhaled from her boots. Tim was in meltdown now, flapping around the room like the ciggy police were about to burst in, but I ignored him. Tim was a non-smoker. On summer holiday coach trips to Rhyl and Barry Island, Mum and I always sat together in our cloud of smog. It was a vice we shared. Now my mum was dying, and if she wanted a smoke, I was going to make sure she had one.

The next day Annette, who had been a nurse all her adult life, took mum home to look after her. It would not be for long. She died three months later at just fifty-eight years old. The last few weeks were tough on her, so our sadness at her passing was tinged with relief. Of course, I knew better than anyone that she was living on somewhere and no longer in any pain, and I would like to think that this knowledge was some comfort to the others. I understood it was the best thing for her, and I was fine with that - until the day of the funeral.

Because the family knew about my beliefs, they expected a calm and stoic reaction from me on the day. In all honesty so did I. We all overlooked one simple truth. No matter how sure a person is that their deceased loved one is living on somewhere, at peace and free of pain, it does not detract from the very real sense of loss that they feel. Everyone misses the physical presence of that person in their lives.

When the day of the funeral came I arrived at Annette's house, where uncles and aunts were already gathering. Floral tributes lined the entrance and mourners I had never met were 'sorry for my loss'. Mum's sisters, usually animated, were seated quietly awaiting the cars. The silence was uncomfortable.

"I can't be doing with all these miserable faces." I blurted out to the room. Glancing through the window I remembered the pub over the road that I had earmarked when I parked the car.

"I'm going for a pint! Come and get me when the cars come."

A gasp went up and a chorus of people shouting my name and informing me that I couldn't do that called after me as I crossed the narrow road. I ordered a pint of bitter and chose a vacant table in the corner. Five minutes passed and the door opened. Tim ordered a pint and sat in silence beside me. A minute or two later the door opened again and Uncle Bill, my mum's elder brother joined us. He watched through the heavy crimson drapes for the funeral cars to arrive.

"Time to go lads." He tapped Tim on the shoulder.

We quickly drained our glasses and stood to leave. I reluctantly followed the others onto the street.

Outside Annette's front door stood a hearse. Pallbearers were putting flowers around the coffin. The coffin! I'm not sure why but I was almost surprised to see it. Was mum really in there? Of course not. She had moved on. In that box was the broken shell she stepped out of, just her old overcoat. Still, it made it real somehow. She was gone from us. I broke down and wept inconsolably.

Travelling with my siblings to and from the funeral, all I did was sob. I sobbed all day and nothing anyone said would comfort me. It was the worse day of my life. Despite all I knew about life after death, when it came down to it, I just missed my mum.

For some reason best known only to the powers that be, it is highly unusual for mediums to see anything for themselves. I suppose the gifts we are given are exclusively to help others. Whether it is advice, healing or seeing our loved ones in spirit, it tends not to happen for us, so I was not expecting ever to see my mum again, at least not until it was my turn to join her. Two weeks after her passing, however, I was blessed with the wonderful gift. I saw her one last time, and there was no one more astonished than I.

I have always nurtured an interest in politics, and in particular, the Labour Party, since Malcolm X visited my hometown of Smethwick in 1965 when I was eleven. The American Muslim minister and human rights activist had come to witness for himself the atrocious racism being practised in the British West Midlands, the likes of which rivalled the race riots of the other Birmingham, Alabama in 1963. There were colour bars in pubs and clubs, and black residents were being prevented from buying houses. He came to see for himself and was shamefully verbally abused on the streets. The Tory MP Peter Griffiths had won his parliamentary seat with the slogan, 'If you want a n****r for a neighbour, vote Labour.' This disgusting campaign, along with my Welsh mining ancestry, made me vow to vote labour as soon as I was old enough. Sure enough, when I turned eighteen, I joined the Labour party. It occurred to me that there was a link of sorts between a person's politics and their spirituality. Some people followed the money and what policies would make them better off, while others championed the underdog and supported ideas which did not necessarily benefit themselves but which promoted an equal society.

Malcolm X was possibly the most influential civil rights activist of his time. He was shot dead in New York just nine days after this visit.

In October 1979, just two weeks after the death of my mother, I was chosen to be a delegate at the Labour party conference in Brighton. Local MP Peter Archer QC asked me to book him a room in the hotel where I was staying, all expenses paid. I was very excited, and probably the keenest delegate there. I took my seat to watch every step of the conference from 9 am to 6 pm each day. My speech was on education. By now I was somewhat accustomed to speaking publicly, although even to this day I am always apprehensive before walking on stage. It crossed my mind that one way to change the world for the better might be to enter politics rather than the church. I toyed with the idea for some time but concluded that I had been born with psychic ability for a reason, and the chances were that therein was the key to my intended path.

By Thursday evening, back in my hotel room, I was buzzing. It had been a thoroughly enjoyable week. I threw back the mustard candlewick bedspread, put one leg between the crisp, freshly starched sheets then stopped. I must have left the window open. The net curtains and velour rust drapes were suddenly billowing into the room, lifted by a gale-force wind. I moved to close it but before I could there was my mum, clear as crystal, hovering by the foot of my bed.

She smiled.

"You know I am ok and happy. Tell the others."

I wanted so much to talk to her, but before I could open my mouth, she was gone. The curtains were still now, and when I crossed the room to close the window, I found it already tightly shut. I have never seen my Mum since, and I have never known anyone else 'blow in' through the window in that way. It was a bittersweet and unique experience that I will never forget.

Moat Farm Infant School. I am third from the left, front row.

A day at the seaside

A trip to Gretna Green with Mum. She cried when the piper played Amazing Grace

Left to right, me, Helen, Annette and Tim

Annette and Jeff. Next to them is Helen, then Auntie Ella, (who liked her tea leaves read). Helen's husband Barry is at the back. Tim and Mum are next to Ella and I stand in front of them.

Malcolm X visits Smethwick

Astral Travel

The Birmingham Pub Bombings

Blue Cloud

Prayer Stones at Aberdaran

Pepe

Yeung

4
Medium Rare

Soon after the death of my mother I experienced an intense yearning to return to her native Wales, the land of song and poets, where mountains dip their feet in the ocean and green valleys cup their palms to drink. I knew it was time to make a dramatic change in my life. My heart told me that my old spiritual home would be the perfect place to start.

I continued to give healing and readings in the West Midlands, and I took the church service from time to time. Periodically I held public demonstrations of mediumship in the local community centre and occasionally larger venues such as Digbeth Civic Hall. It seemed a tide of interest was rising, and as word got around a nagging voice was telling me I wasn't doing enough. By now I was area manager for the Lo-Cost Supermarket group, which took up a great deal of my time, meaning my 'psychic work' had been demoted to an afterthought, fitted in only as and when. Like a woodpecker drumming in my chest, my heart was telling me I should be doing spiritual work full time, but my head would tell me I needed to eat! It was all very well for those in spirit impressing upon me that I needed to be doing more, but I couldn't see how it was practical. I should probably have kept the faith and made the transition of my own volition. Eventually, my hand was forced when I was rendered redundant. I suppose it was the push I needed, and rather suspect it was orchestrated that way. After a week or so of deliberation, I took the decision to become a professional psychic medium. I would make the commitment and devote my life to this work, but I would have to charge people. I wrestled with this idea for a while before realising that even priests and vicars get paid for their work. I concluded that there was no shame in making a living from a vocation and resolved to charge those who could afford it, but vowed I would not turn anyone away if they needed help and did not have the means to pay.

It felt like the right time to make a change. I found a cosy two up, two down cottage in North Wales, very close to a traditional village pub called The Valentine. It was an intimate, coastal community, a far cry from the industrial drone of the West Midlands. The settlement was cossetted between the small protective mountain and a secluded beach, which was a five-minute stroll from my front door. The post office and police station were small houses that had been half-heartedly converted, and the River Dulas, which was little more than a good size stream at this point, trickled close to the main road. It seemed the world turned more slowly in this sleepy little place.

After a short settling in period, I was all set to build my new life. The prospect of using my gifts to help people full-time excited me. I knew I was on the right track. In the beginning, I suspect I was viewed as a somewhat strange addition to the village. In those days pubs were the heart of the community, and I was soon to be put through my paces by the regulars of the two locals. I had never encountered hostelries like them. A cockerel jumped on the bar to call time each night; customers often had to serve themselves, and I learned that the sound of a doorbell ringing in the tap room meant that someone had lifted the fig leaf which protected the modesty of a well-endowed Greek statue in the lady's toilet. One evening in The Valentine the questions came thick and fast. Where had I come from? What did I do for a living? Answering the latter required a deep breath. What would these down to earth people make of my unconventional profession? They would know soon enough, so I tried to look casual, and I told them. There were a few exchanged glances before an old timer seated alone broke the silence.

"What a load of bollocks!"

He took a swig of his mild, and the brass plate which hung on the wall behind him fell and cracked him square on the head. The whole pub fell about laughing, and I was at that moment accepted.

My next step was to work out how to begin in a place where I was completely unknown. Booking a venue seemed like the place to start so I looked around the area for something suitable. The Prince of Wales Theatre in Colwyn Bay seemed to fit the bill perfectly, so I decided to make some enquiries. At sunset I took a short walk to the beach and settled on a rock, allowing my mind to ebb and flow like the waves around me. I tasted the salt on my lips and watched the foam turn pink with the sky. Surely this must be God's country? As the sea breeze flapped around my ears, it brought with it Blue Cloud's voice.

"There will be obstacles. No one said this would be easy. You will need broad shoulders and a sense of humour."

I listened to the waves until the sky turned grey, then took a stroll home.

The next morning was a glorious summer's day, and I left the cottage with a spring in my step. At the venue, I sought out the theatre manager to see what dates were free. He explained that there were lots of nights available, but I had to go to the Civic Centre to make the booking. Happy to be making progress in my venture I headed over there as though the world was waiting for me.

Stepping out of the sun and into the civic offices, the atmosphere turned instantly cool - in more ways than one. A man in a green overall directed me to a council member, who listened to my request with all the warmth of an Easter Island statue. When I had finished, he informed me that this was not the sort of thing they would wish to see at the 'Prince of Wales'. I pointed out with all the courtesy I could manage, that people should be able to decide for themselves what they wanted to see and that if they didn't wish to come to my evening, then surely they wouldn't buy tickets? My words carried zero leverage, and I was shown the door with all the grace of a schoolboy caught smoking in the music cupboard. As I made for the exit the councillor followed me, muttering, "I have seen this sort of thing get out of hand," (I very much doubted it), "and I'm not happy that you intend to charge people either!"

The door slammed, with my suggestion to let me hire the theatre for free so that I wouldn't need to charge people, still hanging in the air. Demoralised I made my way home - via the pub.

Two days later a letter arrived from the council's director of amenities. 'After consultation with the committee members, your application for hire of the theatre is not granted.'

That afternoon I received an interesting phone call from the local press who had heard of my rejection and no doubt smelled the potential of an article slightly more interesting than the local bake sale. They embraced the story for the fiasco it was and honoured it with such headlines as, 'Clairvoyant Told There is no Future for his Show' and 'Spiritualist Barred from Council Theatre.' I chose to take the attitude that any publicity had to be good. I had moved to an area where I was relatively unknown. At least now people would know I was here.

Fuelled by frustration and the power of stubborn determination I resumed my search. The Aberconwy Centre on Llandudno's promenade was my next choice, and thankfully the management were more receptive than the council had been. I booked a date a couple of months ahead, placed some adverts in the local paper, had some tickets printed and I was up and running!

I was confident until three days before the big night when my nerves began to jangle. I called into the theatre, only to find they had sold a paltry sixteen tickets! The manager made re-assuring noises, explaining that often people didn't book in advance but tended to turn up on the night. I hoped and prayed he was right. The theatre seated nine hundred people and sixteen occupied chairs would look rather silly.

Tim travelled down from the West Midlands in a show of support and offered to introduce me onto the stage. I also needed someone to take appointments on the night in case anyone wanted to book a reading. I had met a pretty young lady called Diane on my travels. She agreed to do the job in exchange for free admission. Everything was in place. All we needed now were bums on seats.

I arrived early on the night, walking to the dressing room past the empty rows with my heart in my mouth. This had the potential to be the most embarrassing event of my life! Soft music was piped into the hall, and Tim went to fetch a pint of mild for me from the bar for Dutch courage.

Twenty minutes passed. I could hear murmuring and shuffling, so I took a peep into the auditorium. Thankfully people were arriving in a respectable quantity. As the time for curtain up crept ever closer I suddenly realised that I had not seen Diane to give her my diary.

"Get out there Tim, and find Diane!"

He pointed out that he had no idea what this girl looked like or where to find her.

I was unsympathetic. "Just find her and give her this!"

I thrust the diary into his hands, and shoved him through the curtains. The room began to hush as the crowd noticed a presence on stage. Tim clumsily took the microphone from its stand, causing thumps and whistles to bounce off the walls.

"Good Evening. Um, is there a Diane in the room?"

A young lady with dark hair raised her hand and the audience began to applaud, slowly at first then more enthusiastically. I realised what was happening and put my head in my hands.

"No, no! I'm not David", the horror told in Tim's voice. "It hasn't started yet!"

I held my breath then burst out laughing as he scuttled red faced back into the dressing room. It was probably the best cure for my nerves I could have wished for. When I walked onto the stage a few minutes later to see an expectant five hundred people all staring at me, I was calm, focused and ready to give this my best shot.

At the back of the theatre, a smart middle aged woman was arriving late, shaking her umbrella and settling into her seat.

"The lady on the back row – in the raincoat." I began. She looked left and right then nervously back in my direction. "Yes, that's right" I continued. "I have a red haired lady called Hilda with you, and a man whose name was John but people knew him as Jackie." No response. "With the lady is a large black Labrador. She is holding a brooch that she left for you, and she says her mother was Ivy." Nothing. Just a puzzled expression. This was going down well! "Don't you know any of these people?"

"Oh yes my Love," she spoke at last, "but they're all dead!"

A giggle rippled through the room. I have no idea what the poor lady thought she was coming to. Perhaps she just came in to shelter from the rain. She was obviously very confused, so I moved on with a smile.

Seated in the aisle a young woman of around thirty sat oblivious to the little girl in spirit who pulled relentlessly at her arm. From the moment I started to describe the child, with her blonde hair, big blue eyes and pretty pink dress, the young lady cried softly into a tissue. I told her that she looked around seven or eight and her name was Nicky or Vicky. The link was not perfect, rather like listening to a crackly old radio. Her mother managed a nod. Then the little girl told me to tell her mum that Danny did it. I passed on the cryptic message and left the young woman to her tears.

On the second row was an elderly lady with a green, woolly cardigan and a face like a bull mastiff waiting to be fed. A gentleman in spirit stood patiently behind wearing a trilby and a tweed jacket.

"I want to come to the lady here." I pointed in her direction. "Forgive my pointing," (my mother always taught me it is rude to point.) "There is a gentleman who would like to talk to you." I went on to describe him then, at last, heard the name Frank. "Can you place who Frank is?"

"Tell him to buggar off!" Her response took me by surprise. "That was my husband. He never spoke to me when he was here, what does he want to talk to me now for?"

The room erupted with laughter. When it quietened, I told her almost apologetically what he had to say, and despite her initial protestations, she seemed pleased with her message in the end.

When it was time for the interval, I was more than thankful. Public demonstrations always drain me, but this time, it was as if I had done five rounds with Mohamed Ali. Tim had a pint ready for me in the dressing room, so I sat and swigged at it as I tried to recoup. I had announced that Diane would be taking appointments for private readings during the interval, and she had taken her seat at a small round table in front of the stage.

I spoke to Tim, "Have a look to see if anyone is booking to see me."

He peered through the curtains. "Come and look at this! I can't believe it! They are queuing right down the aisle. It will take you forever to see all these people!"

I jumped from my seat to look, then laughed until I choked! There was the huge line of people, all queuing - for ice-cream!

The second half went well and as the theatre emptied I retired to the bar, exhausted. Tim and I were ordering beers when the young lady who had lost the little girl tapped me on the arm. Close up I could see there was a striking resemblance between the two.

"I just wanted to say thank you. Nicky was my daughter." Her face was mottled from the aftermath of tears.

"She was murdered."

It was a horrific story. The poor woman had arranged for her cousin to babysit one evening while she went out to celebrate a friend's birthday. When she returned home, she couldn't understand why the house was empty. She went room to room shouting his name and eventually noticed something sticking out from behind the couch. She peered over the top and found her daughter's broken body. The cousin whom she trusted had assaulted and murdered her. As she spoke, I could not imagine how anyone can survive such a horrific loss. She was thanking me for the comfort I had given her in knowing the little girl was living on and could still be with her, but it seemed such small comfort to me. I wished I could undo all the heartbreak and just bring her home to her mum.

As we drove home that evening I was drained, but satisfied that the night had gone well. I hoped I had shown the five hundred or so people that there is nothing to fear in dying, and that I perhaps comforted a few. Several had made appointments to see me privately for a more in depth reading or spiritual healing. As the moon followed us home, I thought of the events of the last few weeks and remembered Blue Cloud's words. I understood now what he meant. I had already found the need for broad shoulders and a good sense of humour and things were only just getting started.

A week or so after my North Wales debut I received a call from a flustered young man named Gary who had read about me in the local paper. He was tripping over his words but managed to explain that he hoped I could help him concerning some poltergeist activity at a flat in Prestatyn, where he lived with his girlfriend and baby. The nineteen-year-olds were petrified by the bumping, banging and scratching sounds they heard each night in the early hours.

He was obviously shaken. "I am sure everyone thinks this is a childish prank, but it's a real nightmare! Things are moving around the flat, and we keep seeing a grey, misty figure in the bedroom doorway."

I arranged to meet him at the flat to assess the situation, and he thanked me enthusiastically. "We don't scare easily, but there's definitely some kind of presence there. Even the baby feels it. He's very unsettled, and the dogs are terrified. They hide away and bare their teeth when the noises start."

The teenagers had initially phoned the police, who found no logical explanation for the happenings and left the building looking rather spooked. Their next step had been to get in touch with two local vicars in the hope that they would exorcise any spirits. Nothing had helped.

The next evening I set off to Prestatyn and found their address easily. There was a parking space right outside the three-story, red brick building. I climbed the stone steps and rang the bottom bell. After a few moments a slim, pale girl showed me in and I followed her up three flights of stairs to the top floor apartment. A small baby was sleeping soundly in a pram in the hallway. The lofty Victorian lounge had been decorated in typical student fashion, with an eclectic mix of classic and bohemian decor. Two young men welcomed me in. One introduced himself as Gary, and the other was a friend who had come to stay with them after the strange happenings began.

We drank coffee and chatted for some time. I explained that poltergeist activity could either be attached to the place or a person living there. On the other hand, if it was rattling pipes I advised them I was no good at plumbing. They told me the background of the story as we waited for someone to communicate. I explained that I could not call anyone up, and we would have to be patient to see if anyone wanted to speak to us. The youngsters talked about cold spots in the flat, of things being moved without explanation and the pram bouncing up and down of its own volition. Locked doors were heard to bang and the noises, which included footsteps running in the empty corridor outside the bedroom, were now also occurring during the daytime. They were quite obviously at their wit's end, to the extent that they had applied to the council for rehousing. I reassured them that they would not be hurt, except in the unlikely event of coming into contact with one of the flying objects of course.

I drank coffee after coffee and walked around the flat for probably a couple of hours before I was aware of any uninvited presence at all. Then, as the teenagers spoke, I noticed their icy breath taking form in the half light. The atmosphere had suddenly changed. My attention turned to the hallway where a tall, slim nurse stood, wearing a white collared, long navy-blue dress gathered in at the waist with a pale blue belt. She looked around sixty years old with dark, but greying hair pulled back severely into a bun. One hand was resting on the pram as she leant over it. I raised my hand to hush the others and asked if they could see her. When they turned towards the hall, they said they could see a faint misty cloud billowing in the area where she stood. As they answered she lifted her head and looked me straight in the eye through tortoiseshell-rimmed glasses. I smiled, and her expression changed. She seemed startled that I could see her.

I conversed with her gently for a short while and in due course, I felt her relax, and she opened up to me a little. She explained that she worked in this building (present tense) and that the others had been ignoring her each time she tried to give them advice when the baby cried. Her demeanour was strict but not unkind. It was clear that she hadn't grasped the reality of the situation and did not realise that she was dead, and had been for probably around a hundred years. I discovered that she didn't believe in life after death, which was most likely why she could not come to terms with what had happened to her. When she rocked the pram, she was trying to lull the baby to sleep and certainly did not mean any harm despite how frightening it all seemed. The rattling of the doors had just been to check they were safely locked, a habit she apparently developed while living on Earth. She was protective of the family and did not want them to move away, although when I told them, they drew little comfort from this fact.

The nurse and I talked well into the night, as I tried to help her understand that she had become earthbound and belonged to the spirit world where she would learn and progress. Blue Cloud and my other helpers played their part in her transition. First, they gained her trust and then they stood in the light so that she would feel comfortable there. Other faces more familiar to her came to help her cross over to the place where she should have been since the moment she passed on. They coaxed and reassured her until she felt ready to let go of her old life.

When at last she had gone into the light, I explained to the young family that they would not be bothered by her anymore and that everything would be okay. It had been a long night, and we were all ready for sleep.

Although the disturbances did stop, Gary and the family remained nervous and were reluctant to stay in the property. They moved out soon afterwards and contacted me some weeks later to say they had discovered that the building was once a house with a large nursery and subsequently a doctor's surgery before it was made into flats.

Word of my Prestatyn ghostbusting efforts spread across North Wales and the number of letters and phone calls I received gathered pace. I learned to prioritise, seeing the people who needed my help ahead of the ones who were only looking to satisfy their curiosity. I concluded another public event might be a good way to reach lots of people at once and perhaps reduce my backlog.

On journeys to and from the young family's home, I had driven by a promising looking venue, the Nant Hall Hotel. It was a magnificent listed building, standing back in its own grounds. The Victorian architecture was spectacular, but its largest room would only seat one hundred people. I went ahead and booked it for two consecutive evenings and decided to experiment with the format, this time, inserting a question and answer forum and also making time for some spiritual healing live on stage.

Both of the evenings proved popular, and they certainly provided a learning curve for me. At one point a queue of people in spirit formed on stage as they waited patiently for their turn. There was a girl called Peggy, an Uncle Bill, a lady called Clara who used to read tea leaves and a twenty-one year-old named Andrew, whose grandmother was in the audience. He had taken his own life, leaving his poor family confused and distraught. The young man was reluctant to tell me why he had done such a desperate thing but did seem eager to let his gran know that it really was him, and he was alright now. He told me that she had his watch and that she kept it by his photograph on the mantle. This seemed to comfort her, but I was sorry I could not get more answers from him. At the end of the first half, the only person unclaimed from the line was a little girl who looked around five years old, who was now playing in the aisle and would not stay still long enough for me to pinpoint who she was with.

After the interval, I asked if anyone present was sick or in pain and would like to receive some healing. At first, the crowd seemed nervous and were reluctant to speak out. A light appeared above the head of a lady near the back. "The lady there with the auburn hair!" I pointed in her direction, but she didn't respond. "The lady behind the tall gentleman in black." Nothing. My vision began to blur. "Have you got a problem with your eyes?"

"Do you mean me Love?" The elderly lady waved at me, – with her white stick! I felt ridiculous and had to stifle a smile as I sheepishly went down to help her up onto the stage and into a chair. Placing my hands on her head I tried to relax so that the healing power could flow. A few minutes had passed before I noticed my hands had begun to slide slowly forwards. To my horror, I realised that she was wearing a wig which was now gradually slipping down over her eyes.

"I can't see at all!" she shouted out to the room. Chairs shuffled, and I turned pink and gradually slid my hands backwards, not wanting to expose her secret to the crowd. The wig fell back into place.

"I can see, I can see!" she cried out. I never did healing on stage again.

When the evening was over, I made my way to the hotel bar where people were waiting to talk to me. Predictably I was both physically and mentally depleted and planned to take a moment to re-group before engaging with anyone. This was not to be, however, as a fair, stocky man in his mid-thirties made straight for me. His dainty, red-haired wife followed, head down, at his heels.

"The little girl you described playing in the aisle," he took my sleeve, "it sounds like our daughter Jenny. Can you tell me what she had to say? Is she alright? We were too nervous to say anything."

Unfortunately, this kind of situation does arise from time to time. People too shy to speak out miss a precious opportunity. When she was there, I could have talked with her, worked on the link and tried to draw her out. Now she was gone, from my view at least, and I don't have a hotline to the spirit world. I am just the telephone between worlds. I cannot call anyone up. More than anything I felt sorry for the little girl who had tried to make contact. There was nothing I could do now except tell her parents that she looked happy and that she had been with them.

Following my move to the North Wales coast, I had many calls and letters from people who used to see me professionally when I was in the West Midlands, mostly asking when I would be back in the area. I would tell them I had no immediate plans to return, until I received an invitation to attend a 'Psychic Fair' in Walsall. Having no idea what a Psychic Fair was, I made some enquiries and discovered it was to be an event where clairvoyants hire a table in a hall and see people individually to give readings. There would also be book stalls, lectures and things of general interest to those intrigued by the many facets of psychic phenomena. It sounded rather crass, but being inexperienced in how to earn a living from my gifts, I was tempted enough to give it a whirl.

I travelled to the Midlands the day before the event and opted to stay overnight with Tim, who by now lived with his wife Rita in Warley. Early the next morning he dropped me at the venue with the promise to collect me at five o'clock.

Stepping into the hall clutching my Marks & Spencer carrier bag my heart sank. I thought for a moment I had joined the circus. All around the room were elaborate stalls in various states of assembly. Silver stars and glittered paint spelt out names such as 'Madame Zola', and 'Sugar & Spice'. I glanced at the door as the organiser approached me but as Tim had already left, there was nowhere to run. The man directed me to a pasting table bearing my name scribbled on a curly yellow post-it.

I reluctantly pulled up two chairs and placed them either side of the table, plonking myself into one of them before rooting through my bag for the red linen table cloth I had thrown in as an afterthought. When I raised my head, a chubby lady in a crimson headscarf and lots of gold jewellery was beaming at me from the other chair.

"Your first time Dearie? Never mind, we'll show you what to do." She jumped up and offered her hand. "Call me Zola."

I introduced myself with a smile and looked at my watch. This was going to be a long day!

"Stan, STAN! Over here! Come and meet David. It's his first time." She was shouting to a skinny guy sporting a droopy, seventies moustache, who was busy erecting fairy lights around the Sugar & Spice sign. He climbed down and wandered toward me with an air of superiority.

"Alright Lad?" His accent had a whiff of Yorkshire. "Me and the missus will help you out if you need any tips." He nodded toward a busty woman, presumably 'Sugar', who was trying to light a twisty gold candle. "Don't expect too much today Son. Next time you can get yourself a proper stand sorted, then you'll do better. Don't be disheartened."

I could not under any circumstance envisage acquiring all the bells and whistles and permanently joining this sideshow. All I had ever done was sit there and just say what I saw.

Behind me, a well-built lady in a long dress and streaky purple hair was erecting a small sign that read simply 'Astrology'. My opinion of astrology in this kind of scenario is not great. While I believe there can be some credibility to the alignment of stars and their influence when studied and charted accurately, I do not accept generalised, all Scorpios are going to meet a tall, dark stranger this week, more commercial kind of astrology.

Her chair backed up to mine, so when I went to the bar for a pot of tea I fetched her a cup to be polite. Just after ten o'clock, people began to drift in and wander around the stalls. I was taking a sip of tea when a voice over my shoulder startled me.

"Hey Lovey, what star sign are you?" Purple lady was obviously quite proactive.

"Um, Leo." A bemused girl answered.

"Could have told you that! Good head of hair! Come here and I'll tell you some more."

Having nothing better to do, I leant back in my chair to listen. The girl made herself comfy and offered her upturned palm which the astrologer took - despite not being a palmist.

"Oh, my word! I don't believe it! In a previous life, you were Joan of Arc!"

This was good stuff! I couldn't believe it. Imagine meeting the person who used to be Joan of Arc! The young lady spent around ten minutes at the table, paid and then left.

I was on my second cup before the next instalment.

"Hey, Lovey, what star sign are you?"

"Libra." This time, it was an older lady.

"I could have told you that. Come and sit down, I'll tell you some more."

The lady sat, and I rolled my eyes.

"Heaven's above! I have never seen anything like this before. Did you know in a previous life you were Joan of Arc?"

I didn't know whether to burst out laughing or tell her what I thought. As it happened, an elderly lady sat down in front of me at that moment, and I was grateful for the distraction.

"You look more like and estate agent than a medium, young man," she had a twinkle in her eye, "I was expecting a long frock and dangly earrings!" I joked that I only wore those on a Saturday night, and went on to tell her what I saw.

She seemed pleased with the messages that came through for her. I said that I should not really predict the gender of daughter's baby, but added that she should start knitting in blue. I explained that the long awaited house move would come in the next month and that her mother Mary in spirit was telling me that she was proud of how she had recovered well from the major operation. She said her daughter was a fighter and that even though she was in the spirit world she had been with her throughout her illness. After the reading, the lady explained she had undergone a double mastectomy when she was just a young woman and that reconstructive surgery had not been possible. That must have been a huge trauma for her. "I'm so sorry," I told her as she squeezed my hand.

Her head tilted with a puzzled expression, then she smiled. "But it's a wonderful thing," she said, "I'm very lucky. It saved my life!"

She left me with a peck on the cheek before hurrying off to tell her friends about the reading.

A young man immediately took her place across the table, followed by an older man and then another lady, who offered me her palm and said, "I'm Scorpio!" I twisted the move into a handshake and replied, "I'm David."

Before long I was yearning for a caffeine fix, specifically a strong cup of tea, but the opportunity to escape my seat was proving elusive. When the last lady got up to leave, I watched for my moment and stood up with her. Like a flash, an old dear took her place.

"I was just going to get some tea." I apologised, knees bent, frozen to the spot.

"Oh," she said, "No need. My friend will fetch it; you sit down." Then she turned to a frail looking woman on the newly formed row of seats behind her. "Ivy! Bring a pot of tea for him while I have a sitting, or we'll be here all day!"

I slowly melted back into my chair and took in a row of around twelve people seated down the middle of the hall, realising with some trepidation that it was a queue to see me. I always feel drained after a reading, and I had never seen so many people consecutively without a break. I could only hope my spiritual batteries would hold out.

As the lady's deceased father randomly told me about his daughter's problem with her car, my eyes danced around the other stands. Madame Zola was finishing off with a young woman, and the other stalls were deserted. I also noticed I seemed to be attracting some rather venomous stares, especially from Sugar & Spice, whose names seemed increasingly inappropriate. I could see that purple astrology lady had packed up and was already heading for the door.

When Tim came to collect me at half-past four, he found me still working my way down the queue which was not getting any shorter. He scribbled numbers on some scraps of paper then went down the line giving out tickets so the people could move around or go to the bathroom without losing their place. He politely suggested that the wait could be a long one, and perhaps they would be better to see someone else, but they were undeterred. They were happy to wait. I, on the other hand, was dizzy, exhausted and longing to go home.

The stall holders were packing up their trappings and loading their cars. Tim heard a few of them complaining they had not taken enough money to cover their costs. As I gave my last reading of the day the hall was empty apart from Tim and a caretaker sweeping up glitter and fluff. On the drive home I thought about how people had not been taken in by all the paraphernalia but had perhaps seen that one little guy with only a table in front of him was, if nothing else, genuine.

As the motor hummed and the windscreen wipers beat time, my thoughts drifted to the lovely lady with the mastectomy. She had such a positive attitude. There are times when your frame of mind can actually determine your quality of life. Those with privileged lifestyles can still be depressed. Many wealthy and well-loved people have committed suicide in their darkest days, and those with mountains to climb can do wonderfully well if they have the right attitude. It is all a matter of perception. If you close your eyes you can put yourself in any situation that gives you peace and contentment. Imagine yourself in a favourite place, perhaps lying on a sunny beach. Think of the sounds, the smells and how you feel when you are there. You will feel as relaxed and peaceful as if you actually are.

The power of thought is an amazing thing. If you think lucky, you will be lucky. Positive thoughts draw positive things. When we walk into a room and can't remember why, we should not say to ourselves, "I don't know what I came here for," but rather, "Why did I come here?" Ask yourself the question rather than make a negative statement, then the answer will come to you. Thoughts are crucial. When we blow out the candles on our birthday cake, we are practising this age old concept. We concentrate on something that we want, focus our thoughts on the candle and blow it out. Another example is the dandelion clock. Where some see a weed others see a wish. If you visualise your goals constructively, it will help you to achieve them, from a simple parking space to a house move or successful career.

Superstition and curses are only born from the power of thought. Curses cannot hurt you unless you believe they can. If you entertain the idea that bad things will happen, you are engaging in negative thought, and this can draw further negativity to you - a self-fulfilling prophecy, as it were. This is why chain letters and emails are so wicked. It is all down to the power of suggestion. 'If you don't send this to ten other people then terrible things will happen'. Of course, this is rubbish – unless you believe it. That negative thought can influence your actions and expectations and attract negativity to you if you take the idea on board.

At Tim's house, I fell asleep thinking about this scenario, and when I awoke, I decided that the Psychic Fair scene was not for me. I had committed myself to one or two more events around the country, but I decided when they were over I would put the whole thing down to experience and resolved to distance myself from this kind of fiasco in the future.

Back in Wales I was approached by the Marina Hotel, which was situated on the promenade in Rhyl. Attached to the hotel was a night club called Celebrities. The manager's wife had seen me at the Aberconwy Centre, and as a result wanted me to hold an evening of clairvoyance at the club. This kind of venue would be a first for me. It was laid out in a cabaret style, with drinks served at the tables. Lots of mediums refuse to work where there is drinking and smoking, but I speculated that going into unusual settings could be the key to reaching people who might not go to a Spiritualist Church.

I had some posters printed and approached a local radio station, who agreed to an interview. This way people who had never been to this kind of evening would know what to expect. It promised to be an interesting and unusual night.

At home, as I was changing into my suit in readiness for the demonstration, my telephone began to ring downstairs. I answered, still adjusting my tie and was shocked to find it was the police.

"This is Chief Inspector Bryant. We have had intelligence which indicates if you go ahead with your meeting tonight your life may be in danger."

There was a long silence as I considered which particular friend might be involved in this kind of wind up. I went along with it for now. "In danger from who?"

"Born again Christians Mr Drew. They consider what you are doing to be 'the work of the devil' and we have been informed they will use whatever means necessary to put a stop to it. They have threatened to slash tyres and even use violence if that is what is required to stop you from going on stage. You might wish to consider calling the evening off."

This was all so far-fetched. "Christians? Are you sure? Surely Christians wouldn't threaten anyone?"

The Chief Inspector seemed convinced. "Our sources are reliable I'm afraid. This is a very real threat."

I felt sick to my stomach, partly through fear and partly because it was unthinkable how some people behave in the name of God. I sat down and told him that the evening would be going ahead as arranged. Tickets had been sold, and I was not going to yield to ignorance. He hung up, after assuring me I would need police protection. I stared at my living room walls for a while then lifted the receiver and called him back, to check the call was genuine. Unfortunately, it was.

Driving to the venue an hour or so later my eyes searched the route for assassins. As I neared Celebrities, I could hear shouts as a hoard of placard carriers came into view. They were vehemently warning people not to enter and quoting the passages from the Bible that suited their purpose. I reminded myself that the devil quoted the scriptures to Jesus in the wilderness and found comfort in the thought that I was in good company.

Two police cars patrolled up and down the promenade, and a couple of constables in uniform were on the door. I decided to use the rear entrance and was greeted by two plain clothed police officers who were there to mingle with the crowd. It was like some elaborate nightmare!

I am always nervous when I walk onto stage, and that evening my fear had taken a new turn. However, I was also determined not to let people down - on either side of the veil. Thankfully the audience were equally stubborn and for the most part crossed the lines of protesters to judge for themselves. The dimly lit room was soon full, and my nerves calmed. I knew I had done the right thing.

I always began with a short talk, introducing myself, explaining how I work and in this instance apologising for the drama. As I spoke two gentlemen in spirit stood in silence either side of a Miss Marple type lady on the first table. Presuming they were waiting to speak, I addressed the tweed-clad woman, telling her of a recent house move, a health condition (shown by the grey patch in her aura over her stomach), and various other things I learned from her aura. Still the two men made no attempt to communicate. As I wound up her message, she stood to ask me a question.

"Young man, I've been married twice, and they are both dead. When I die who will I go to?"

 Without a flicker of expression the man on her right said, "She's not coming here!" and the man on her left said, "She's not coming here!"

I smiled to myself. I knew that I couldn't lie, so hoping to be tactful I found my answer.

"You will go to where the love is."

This statement is very true. If there is no love between you and your partner, you will not be together after you pass. Whoever you have that bond of love with will be with you.

Behind Miss Marple, a table full of bubbly young ladies whispered and giggled into their wine glasses. Not all people come to me for help. Some come for entertainment or purely out of curiosity. I don't mind whatever the reason because often the ones who are out for a bit of fun are surprised to find they gain help or understanding nonetheless. A light hovered over the head of a blonde girl on the left so I pointed her out. She smiled and raised her glass to confirm she was listening. As she did so, my face fell, and I instantly regretted the choice.

I am often asked if I tell people the truth of what I see, good or bad. These people are usually unnerved by the answer. I have to trust that spirit are relaying their messages to me for a good reason, so I rely on them entirely and simply tell the truth. That is not to say it is always easy. If I can see that someone is going to have a baby, for example, it is hard to tell if it will be good news or bad. As I looked at this happy, carefree looking girl, my heart was in my mouth. I took a breath and said, "I'm so sorry, but I have to say I am picking up that you only have a matter of months or perhaps a few weeks to live."

Around the room heads turned. People were staring at me now with open mouths. I held my breath. The girl was still smiling but tears now welled in her eyes as she softly said, "Thank you." I could not help becoming emotional. All eyes were on me as my voice cracked. "Don't thank me! I have just told you that you are going to die."

What she said next made me realise why spirit had shown me this. "I know I am dying. If you had told me anything else tonight, I would not have believed in you. Now I know that there is an afterlife and that I don't have to be afraid."

The table of girls were teary eyed now, but managed to be strong for their friend and tried to keep her upbeat. The one seated beside her took her hand as I went on to give the young woman a message from her grandmother and a friend of hers in spirit. That one communication alone made the whole evening worthwhile and justified all the stress that being there had generated. I held my head high that night as I walked past the placard brigade to my car. The next morning I made plans to hold more meetings across the country. I knew that if I spoke to five hundred people and only two accept what I have to say it was still worthwhile.

Just a few days later I took a call from a young woman in nearby Llandudno. She had heard about what I did and asked if I would call to see her at home. Her voice was sad, and I could tell she was in a very dark and emotional state. I took directions and visited her the next evening.

It was a broad, tree lined street. Standing in the well-kept garden, I rang the bell of the large private house. Children's voices rang out from upstairs, and a few moments later the door opened tentatively to reveal an attractive lady with short, dark hair. Over her shoulder, the hazy shape of a man, perhaps in his thirties, stood in the hallway.

She seemed nervous, unsure how to begin, so she showed me into the lounge and left the room to make tea. When she returned the young man behind her was a little clearer. As she placed the cup on the coffee table, I spoke.

"I know exactly why you have phoned me. Have you quite recently lost your husband?"

She froze, startled, then sat on the armchair opposite. Her soft, brown eyes were filling with tears and she couldn't speak for a while, so I just related what he looked like and what he was saying. He told me she was feeling guilty about something, and she must stop this. I was given the impression he had worked in a financial institution, perhaps a bank. His name was Alex.

When she could, the lady introduced herself as Hannah and explained that her husband, who had only passed a few weeks earlier, had worked for the Inland Revenue. He came home from his wine club one evening not feeling well. She told him he was the worse for wear, and he went to bed. When she went up to join him a few hours later, he was unresponsive. She called an ambulance, but it was too late.

I visited Hannah regularly for a while, feeling like a third wheel as husband and wife spoke intimately to each other via me. There was such a strong love bond between them. As time went on our meetings became less frequent, until at last each of them was able to move on and adapt to their new lives in very different worlds.

5
Bricks and Balloons

When death comes to take you, it creeps like a burglar, appearing when you least expect it, even though you know the possibility of its arrival was always there. Life on Earth is very short, even if you live to be one hundred years old. It is like a day at school, and it is not meant to be easy. Like walking up an escalator that is steadily descending it is hard to climb up but so easy to go down. All you have to do is stand still.

There are lessons we need to learn in this life, and things we must experience to help us to progress. Often you will hear people complain that they keep making the same mistakes over again, perhaps in relationships or other walks of life. We are presented with a repeated set of circumstances until we understand where we are going wrong. Like failing an exam, you have to re-sit before you can advance. It makes me sad to hear people say that if there were a loving God, then He would not allow suffering in the world. At five-years-old I wondered why my mum made me go to school when all I wanted to do was stay home with my family. Although I couldn't have comprehended it at the time, it is obvious to me now that she was giving me, out of love, not what I wanted, but what I needed. When God drives us into deep water He is not trying to drown us. He does this to cleanse us. We learn our lessons and then we go home, grateful when the bell sounds that our hard day's work is over, and hopeful we have benefitted from the day's experiences.

We are born into a kind of hedge-maze, and our task is to find the way out. Some people take longer than others to get it right, some die young while others linger, clinging to what they think life is. They are afraid to take that step we must all one day take, and even more afraid to let their loved ones make it. It is perfectly natural to fear the unknown, especially when it seems so scary. The novice skydiver is petrified to make his first jump and may even need a push when the moment comes. He is gripped by fear, but on the way down begins to feel exhilarated. When he lands, he may leap up shouting, "Wow! That was fantastic! What was I afraid of? Let's do it again!"

We all have to make that jump one day, but there is no need to be afraid, and although we will miss our loved ones, there is no reason to fear for them when it is their turn to take that jump. Life is a continuous circle. We are in spirit; we live on Earth and then we return to spirit. There is no death, only different levels of life. Letting go is never easy, but if we are honest, it is ourselves we grieve for when we lose someone. We mourn their presence in our life as they advance to an exciting new dimension leaving us behind.

Ruby was a pleasant, middle-aged lady with an infectious laugh. I met her when she visited me for a private reading at my little stone cottage only a month or so after I moved in. She was pleased with the sitting and afterwards we had a long chat by the fire. She was one of the first people I saw professionally in North Wales.

One spring afternoon around a year later, she telephoned me from Ysbyty Glan Clwyd, a hospital in Denbighshire. She was in a most desperate state. Her twenty-one-year-old son had been involved in a horrific motorcycle accident and was now on life-sustaining apparatus which was breathing for him, keeping him alive. Fighting tears, she told me she could see him breathing, just like he was asleep, but the doctors had told her he was brain stem dead. They were asking her permission to turn off the support. Sitting with him, holding his warm hand, she could not bring herself to give consent. Then she thought of me. There was still some hope in her heart. She would not make her decision until I had seen him.

The sun was warm on my shoulders as I crossed the hospital car park. A murmuration of starlings swooped and climbed, looping ever changing shapes against the blue sky. Life was going on as usual, but inside that building I knew that the world was now a very different place for Ruby.

Standing by her son's bedside with Ruby at my shoulder, I could see without a doubt that his spirit had long since gone. His chest lurched up and down, and his skin was pink, but he had not been in his body for some time. On the bed was the ember of a young man, the shell her boy once occupied. I sat with her at the worst moment of her life and tried to explain.

The soul or spirit is the essence of who we are. It is the thing that loves, feels compassion and decides in us whether we swat the beetle or let it live. I explained that this was just her son's old overcoat on the bed. He didn't need it anymore. He had gone on to another existence, and the silver cord which joins spirit to body was now broken. There was no way his soul could re-enter and live again on Earth.

Because the body is just a vehicle, it is perfectly acceptable, and indeed commendable, to donate organs for transplant, thereby enabling another to live out their life. The decision to do so comes at the most challenging time, but having the understanding that your loved one has already gone perhaps makes it a little easier.

I waited in the corridor as one by one the nurses removed tubes and turned off the machines. Ruby sat with her son as his body gave up, there for him at the end of this life as she was at the beginning. Her heart was broken, but I knew without question that the doctors were right in their judgement.

Science tells us that our brain is programmed to respond to situations in a specific way, fight or flight, procreation of the species and so on, and while this is true, it is certainly not all there is to us. If it were, we would all make identical decisions when faced with the same set of circumstances, yet of course we do not. The mechanics of death is often discussed in such a clinical way, but dying is truly an intimate and very personal experience.

Our brain is just an organ of the body, like the liver or the heart. It is not who we are. When we die, it will rot in the ground but our consciousness lives on, shifting to a different dimension as easily as switching channels on the TV. Like Alice stepping through the looking-glass, it is as simple as walking into the next room. If your partner goes into the bedroom to sleep, you can no longer see him, but you know he is still around somewhere and that this parting is not permanent. When you do see him again, no matter how long it has been, it seems like only a moment since you were in the same room.

We are all composed of a mind, a body and a spirit. The brain is physical and is part of the body. The spirit and the mind make up your real self which is immortal. All your earthly experiences are registered in your brain then transferred to your mind via the silver cord. When you pass over you will remember your life on Earth because the information is stored in your mind.

It may help if you think of this as an invisible rucksack on your back. Throughout your life's journey, you pick up items and throw them into the bag to keep and treasure. You are continually introduced to a wealth of information; some is valuable, and some is worthless. You must choose which to accept and which to reject. This is a crucial exercise. It would be disastrous to reach your destination only find you have a rucksack full of apple cores and crisp packets, and have left all the essentials you need by the side of the road.

It is possible, in exceptional circumstances, to tap into the wealth of knowledge you hold in your mind, gained from previous existences. This hidden hard drive is called your higher self. It is a part of yourself which generally eludes you while you are on the earth. If you find yourself in a difficult situation, then suddenly the solution may just seem to come to you out of the blue. This happens when the knowledge is there within your higher self and you have drawn from it. Perhaps you have experienced similar circumstances in a previous lifetime, and the information is transferred by means of the silver cord from your mind to your brain when it is needed.

Science is a wonderful thing. With study, we can learn how the stars were born, how the human body works and how plants provide the medicine to cure us. As man acquires this knowledge, he thinks himself wise. He does not comprehend that science is God's greatest creation. He is naïve enough to believe that all those feats of engineering and miracles of nature are the products of some huge coincidence orchestrated entirely by chance.

We are housed in our body only for the duration of this life on Earth. It is just an item of clothing for your soul or spirit. Like the deep sea diver needs a heavy suit to walk on the seabed, we need a body to live on the earth. The diving suit connects to the surface with a line, as the body is attached to the spirit with a cord, and when it is time to shake that suit off in both scenarios we experience a huge relief.

In appearance, the silver cord is like a shining rope of infinite length which radiates a pure, silvery blue light. We enter this world at the cutting of a cord, and we leave it when the silver cord breaks. Once it has been severed, there is no going back. You may hear of people on the operating table who died for a while then revived, living to tell stories of the things they saw. A lady called Maggie from Warrington told me that when she was having a hysterectomy, she left her body and was floating in the air looking down at the surgeons. They were panicking. She then felt an intense pain spreading from her stomach to her head, and the next thing she remembered was being back on the operating table. Later in intensive care, she looked down from the ceiling at the nurse who was attending to her. The surgeon later told her that they nearly lost her. Her heart stopped beating, but as she was still joined to her body by the silver cord, it was possible to revive her. This is known as a near-death experience, and in these cases, the cord does not break so the spirit is able to return to the body.

The spirit of an elderly gentleman who has led a good life may slip in and out of his body, still joined by the silver cord as he nears death. He will likely see friends and relatives long gone as they draw near to assist him with his transition. Carers may think the old boy is rambling as he mumbles about his mother or long lost brother, but they truly are there with him and have come to help. As his spirit drifts between these states of spiritual and physical, the silver cord grows thinner and thinner until at last it breaks, his earthly body dies and his family help him over.

Researchers at Hospice Buffalo in Cheektowaga, New York explored the end of life visions of their patients. Their first study was published in The Journal of Palliative Medicine. Fifty-nine terminally ill patients were interviewed and almost all reported having dreams or visions featuring visitations from departed loved ones. One seventy-six year old man 'dreamed' of his mother who died when he was a child. He could smell her perfume and heard her voice saying that she loved him. The doctors are looking for a scientific solution to what these dreams mean, but the answer is a spiritual one. All agree however that patients are usually comforted by these experiences.

In a related and equally extraordinary scenario it is possible for a person's spirit to leave their body whilst they are still alive and not near death. This phenomenon is called astral projection or sometimes astral travel. Only our physical body needs rest, so while we sleep our spirit is free to leave its shackles. Everyone does this from time to time, although you may not always recollect the detail. You could walk around your house wondering why the light switches don't work, or travel in advance to a city you intend to visit, creating the strange sense of déjà vu when you arrive and feel you have been there before.

Even more bizarrely, it is possible, although not common, for you to astral travel at the same time as a friend who lives miles away and then meet up and converse with them. Although you may not remember this, you may wake with that person on your mind, and perhaps telephone them, only to find they were thinking of you too. It is not unheard of for people to see the 'ghost' of someone who isn't dead. This is often dismissed as imagination, but it can be that while that person is asleep their spirit is astral travelling.

A common experience related to astral travel is being awakened with a violent and powerful jerk. This can be rather alarming but is quite safe. It is simply the spirit leaving or returning to your body too rapidly.

It is possible to travel to other dimensions whilst in this state, perhaps being taken to meet with loved ones who are in the spirit world. The silver cord remains intact throughout these experiences, and your spirit returns safely to your body before you wake. Your memory may retain fragments of the experience, but if you fully recalled all that you had seen you could become very dissatisfied with your life.

In the spirit world, there are many planes of existence, each within a different dimension. Jesus simplified this wonderfully when he told us that there are many mansions in His Father's house. Thankfully not everyone who is dead resides in the same place. It would be unthinkable if the executed child murderer went to the same destination as his victim. The manner in which you have lived your life on Earth determines which of these planes will be your home. When I was a young boy, Blue Cloud explained this in a simplified form to help me understand. He spoke of the spirit realm like a block of flats. On the roof of the building is heaven, the earth is the ground floor and the basement represents hell, or the pits as I prefer to call it. Within the building, there are seven higher floors, each of which is occupied by people who are at a similar level of spiritual development. Level one is the first above the earth plane and level seven is the closest plane to heaven. On each floor are rooms, again numbered one to seven. Our goal throughout eternity is to progress through the levels, room by room, floor by floor until we reach heaven. The earth is the training ground, and we must return to it from time to time to receive the lessons we need to absorb if we are to progress. When we go back to the spirit world, we can then be promoted to a higher level. Just as we cannot learn all our lessons in one day at school, we need more than one life on Earth to understand all that is needed in order to progress spiritually. Each time we are born it is into a predetermined set of circumstances, the conditions required to give us the particular experiences we need. For example, if you have always been wealthy, perhaps you may not be able to fully understand that you should have shared your good fortune. It may be that you cannot appreciate what it is like to suffer hardship until you have lived it. If you have racist tendencies, perhaps you will be born into a different culture. We are never forced to come back to Earth, in fact, we have to earn the opportunity. The catch is that having done so, we are born with a clean slate and no recollection of our past or what it is we need to learn. It is possible for someone to come from the second room on the third floor, have a life here then get it completely wrong, only to find when they pass over they are back on the first level or even in the pits. This opportunity is a double or quits gamble, and the ultimate decision to take it is ours.

The earth is a fascinating place. It is the only plane of existence where people of different spiritual persuasions walk around together in the same dimension. This is because it is a place of learning, a journey rather than a destination.

Where we go to in the spirit world is not so much a punishment or reward situation as a product of God's natural laws. Pepe explained this very well to me from the top of the wardrobe one morning as I searched for my shoelace, which I had used to play conkers the day before. Each time we do something good we are presented, metaphorically speaking, with a balloon, and each time we do something wicked or detrimental to others, a brick is hung around our neck. Even our thoughts and words can earn us balloons or bricks. Balloons will help us to soar spiritually high, but bricks will drag us down toward the pits. How many of each we have when we die determines our destiny. Of course, it takes many balloons to lift just one brick. Throughout our lives, we are acquiring bricks and balloons, regardless of our faith or religious beliefs. Repenting in order to be saved is a nice idea, but there is no quick fix. It can certainly be the beginning of a change in your life, but if you repent on your death bed you will still have the bricks or balloons earned during the course of your life, and this will determine your fate. If you think you have never done anyone any harm, it is not enough to save you. You will only get balloons by doing good things for others. God pays His workers well, but not in advance. Someone who has no religious belief but loves his fellow man and lives a good life helping people will still have many balloons. This is God's natural law, because whether you believe in Him or not, He believes in you. Those who disobey God, ignore His teachings or disregard His instruction will weep with sorrow in the darkest realms of the pits. This is not a threat; it is simply the effect of His natural laws. He watches us all and sees the good rise up and the wicked fall down, and if you think you are good then you are not! Be humble, gentle, patient, kind and tolerant. Our Father is a fair and loving God, but He is also a God of justice who hates arrogance. Do not make excuses or blame others for your mistakes. Ask for His forgiveness and He will give you strength, courage and guidance.

People ask me from time to time if their loved one might have reincarnated before they pass over themselves, thereby depriving them of the opportunity to be reunited in the spirit world. This scenario would be highly unlikely. Hundreds of years can pass before someone is offered the chance to have another life. The newly departed pass immediately to a kind of neutral area, where after being re-assured by loved ones, they meet the spirit helpers they never knew they had, and their entire earthly life is then analysed with the help of their spirit guide. This experience can come as a shock, as seemingly inconsequential things you said or did are often revealed to have had a surprising impact, good or bad, on the lives of others. God examines us closely throughout our lives and knows us inside out. He is aware of everything we do, say and even think. His knowledge of us is profound. It is beyond our understanding. He keeps a daily diary of us all, and upon our passing, we will get to see it. After this, your new home is allocated and you are taken to the place where you and your spiritual equals belong.

My first encounter with the concept of reincarnation was in my adolescence. It was during one of my night-time chats with Blue Cloud. I had looked into the Buddhist faith during my exploration of various religions and decided to take the opportunity to question him on the subject. I could think of no-one more qualified to answer than a man who had been dead for four hundred years.

Blue Cloud, or BC as I was calling him by now, confirmed that reincarnation was real, but stressed that people will always be people and animals always animals. Genders, however, can and often do change. This repeated visitation to the planet is a further explanation for the experience of déjà vu. Sometimes we feel familiarity with a place because we lived there in a previous incarnation. It is a rare glimpse into our personal history, which is hidden from us at birth so that we can begin with a clean slate, uninfluenced by our past. Blue Cloud then added a startling revelation. In his last incarnation, in what is now the Winnipeg area of Canada, I was *his* spirit guide! He was on Earth and I was in the spirit world guiding and helping him. It seems he was now returning the favour. It was a mind-blowing concept for a teenager. What is more, just as I am in the unique position of being able to communicate directly with my guide, he was also able to communicate with me when roles were reversed. Native Americans are a spiritual people who actively believe in the spirits of their ancestors. This so-called primitive race is in many ways more spiritually advanced than their 'civilised' but closed minded cousins. This is the reason so many from this race go on to be spirit guides. He added that he can show himself as whichever one of his many earthly lives he chooses.

He added that it is not uncommon for the close friends and loved ones we meet in spirit, to offer to help us when we decide to reincarnate. If they are spiritually high, they may become our guide or helper from the other side, trying to put positive thoughts into our head and point us in the right direction. Alternatively, they might decide to have a life on Earth, alongside us. In this case, your paths are steered so that they cross, in the hope that you feel some affinity with each other. This is a risky scenario which, as you may imagine, can go horribly wrong.

Thinking about his words I realised the spirit guide's job is not an easy one. Having halted all personal advancement for themselves, they whisper in our heads and pray that we take the advice they give, but all too often we do not. Some people refer to this as their conscience, the inner voice that tells us right from wrong.

Everything has an opposite, however, and just as there are those who want to steer you to do the right thing, there are also more sinister influences trying to drag you off course. It is a constant battle between good and evil. The more spiritual you are, the easier it is for those on high to influence you, the more materialistic a person is the more readily they will accept the devil's persuasion. For every thought that inspires you to visit the lonely old dear next door, there is another that tells you she would probably rather not be disturbed, and you would do better to have that well-deserved soak in the bath instead. It all happens in a flash, and your spirituality hangs upon which voice you choose. It is a frightening thought, but once you are aware of this it is easier to avoid the pitfalls. The rule of thumb is that the selfishly motivated thought, is likely to be the wrong one. The right path is usually the hardest. If it is clear that you want to follow God, then the devil and his helpers will be all the more active in trying to throw you off course. He is very sly and will offer you sweeteners. There is a saying, 'the devil comes in the shape of your best friend', and this is very true. That voice that says you deserve to think of yourself more often may sound like a real friend, but he is deceiving you. The next stranger you meet may be secretly influenced to help you, but the devil disguises himself too. He relies on people not believing in him, so that they are off their guard. Reject the advice of those who are influenced by the devil and do not follow their example.

Almighty God watches over those who obey and put their trust completely in Him. Walk with God rather than try to call Him over to you. Do not choose the wrong path and then ask for protection. He will only live in a clean heart. The devil is not so selective. He will live anywhere.

I used to wonder at the reason for these sinister influences. Why does God allow it? Over time I have realised if there was nothing but good in the world, then there would be no accolades for doing the right thing. If there was no choice between good and evil, how could we show God that we love Him by choosing Him over the devil? If there was no wrong answer, then there would be no prize for getting it right. All things must have an opposite. The greatest gift we are given is our free will, and we are at liberty to select our own direction. God may hope we choose His way, but He will not stop you if you decide on a different path. The decision is ours. The Almighty Father is not hiding. His words are more precious than gold, and He will show you what is right and what is wrong, but it is not open for debate. If we get lost it is nobody's fault but our own.

People often ask why God has forgotten them when it is they who have forgotten Him. They walk away from Him then say He has abandoned them. His justice dictates that if we forget what He asks of us, He may just forget what we ask of Him. We cannot say we love God but then not do what we know he expects of us. To do this is hypocritical. We need to be true to ourselves and to Him. We cannot hide from God.

You may think that because I can talk to my guides and helpers that choosing the right pathway is easier for me, but an important part of God's plan is that we make our own choices. Blue Cloud, like any other guide, tries to steer me in subtle ways towards the opportunities that will lead me to my intended pathway, but he will not demand that I take it. Our guides talk to us all the time. People tell me that they wish they could speak to their guide, but anyone can do this. Just because you cannot see them. this does not mean they are not there for you. They influence us, but we are all personally responsible for our actions. This is my life. If I were constantly under orders, there would be no credit for my achievements or blame for my shortcomings. In any case, being more than a little stubborn, I would probably baulk at being told point blank what I must do.

An old, Welsh collier used to joke, "Hello David, how am I?" every time I walked into my local pub, and if I ever trip, the favourite jibe is always, "Ah, you didn't see that coming did you?" It gets a little old but I tend to reply with a smile and a nod like I never heard it before. Of course, there are surprises and mishaps in my life. What I see is for the benefit of others, not myself. I am here on the same terms as everyone else.

At this point in my life, I certainly did not anticipate I was about to be steered toward a situation that would change the course of my life dramatically.

6
Out of the Blue

Love comes in many forms. It twists, rotates and transforms our lives like the pinions in a clock. The love of our parents moulds us, love for our siblings inspires us, for our children it fulfils us but it is the love of a soul mate that completes us. No other love is quite so consuming.

Many of us have soul mates, but that is not to say we walk the land together. If we do, to find one another, let alone share a life on Earth is an exceptional gift.

Over the years I enjoyed (for the most part) numerous romantic relationships. Some lasted days; others went on for years. I will not dwell on these liaisons because they were of little consequence to the direction of my life. They came and went like petals on a stream, delightful but fleeting, and more than once I thought I had loved. Then I met Jane.

You could say it was an unlikely setting, not the romantic location Hollywood would have chosen for the meeting of soul mates, and yet overnight a random, seedy old town entwined itself through my most precious memories like the sweetest of grapevines.

I had been travelling a lot and was working in Blackpool, a tourist town on the Lancashire coast, famous mostly for its fairgrounds and fairy lights. The wind boxed my ears as I hurried from the carpark to the seafront venue where I was booked to appear. To my left, an excavator was demolishing some historical but unattractive building with surprising dexterity. The grabber reached into the gaping hole like a great beast, grasping and extracting a single pole, then a bunch of cables with swift, liquid movements. Promenade arcades and rock shops somehow tainted the raw beauty of the shoreline like lipstick on a child. The red lattice tower was beginning to cast its shadow by the time I had set up and was ready to work.

I began with a talk on life after death and spoke to several individuals before taking my scheduled and extremely welcome twenty-minute break. There were no violins or drumrolls, but I do remember a strange energy in the air as I saw her before me, an unassuming girl around ten years my junior, without guile or glamour. Her windswept dark hair fell about her shoulders, and there was little make-up on the face that now pleaded with me, asking if I could see anything with her. Although I could tell that she was at a crossroads in her life, she carried a surprising air of serenity. As I spoke into her hazel eyes, I suddenly felt I had known them forever. Words dropped randomly from my mouth like marbles to the floor as I hurriedly scribbled my number on the back of a receipt I found in my pocket and invited her to call if I could be of any help.

I was no more searching for love that day than she was. It is strange how we often find the most precious things when we least expect it.

That night I couldn't sleep. What if she didn't call? What if she was gone forever? Why was I obsessing about a girl I met so briefly? When I closed my eyes, I saw her face. Several long days passed before her call finally came. She asked if I was available for a private consultation and I casually fixed an appointment. A few days passed before I visited the home where she was living with her mother, and after the reading, we went for a drink. I called on her the next day, and again the day after that, taking her gifts of jewellery like some lovesick teen. At first, I couldn't understand what was happening to me. Something was drawing me towards this girl, and when she wasn't with me, I felt unexpectedly lost. It was strange to find my independence evaporating into thin air when she wasn't around, and the realisation that I was no longer emotionally self-sufficient floored me. This was a surprising new weakness, yet I knew if she chose to be with me I would have the strength, or at least the enthusiasm to accomplish anything. When I touched her hand for the first time, something seemed to shift beneath our feet. I knew that I needed her. I suspected BC had some hand in this. He had lit the blue touch-paper, and the firework was well and truly alight. I felt restless, as though the stars were aligning in readiness for some huge event.

Friends and family thought I had lost the plot. It must have seemed ridiculous, but I suddenly knew what I wanted, and I was going for it. Without hesitation, I left my prized cottage in Wales and rented a ground floor flat near Blackpool airport just to be near my Jane.

We would walk in the park, holding hands, feeding the ducks and learning how to love each other. It became our special place. I wrote her poetry, and she tried not to laugh. She whispered she loved me, and I tried not to cry. I smoked less and reduced the sugar in my tea to impress her with my healthy lifestyle. I greeted these magical days each morning with the excitement of a child. When I called on her one afternoon and she wasn't home, I made my way to the park, sitting beneath the café's towering Art Deco ceiling. Hot tea steamed up my glasses as I irrationally stared through the giant windows, longing for that flip of my heart when I saw her. She later asked me what my logic was - if I thought she was some vagrant who wandered around the Italian gardens all day. Admittedly all logic had deserted me, and I could not explain my reasoning, other than to say I felt close to her there.

I knew without any doubt that this was the girl I would marry. Within a week of our first meeting I had taken the initiative, gathered all the confidence I could muster and proposed. I remember a seemingly endless pause as I tried to read her expression. Smiling gently, she took my hand, and spoke slowly, taking care with the words she chose.

"From the moment we met I somehow knew the person you are inside." It was strange to her she said, but at the same time so natural. "When I looked into your blue eyes for the first time I wasn't afraid anymore. When I found you, I felt safe. Everything just fell into place."

We were a perfect fit and finding each other was as easy on the heart as coming home. Taking my hand she described how when I spoke, she even somehow knew what I *wasn't* saying. However, being of sound mind she went on to crush me without a second thought. "But Darling, I think we probably shouldn't rush this."

I pushed the argument that I didn't see the point of waiting when I knew we were meant to be together. I told her I thought we should marry soon; I could book a date tomorrow. She smiled, put her arms around my neck and sweetly kissed me before changing the subject.

We married one sunny August morning exactly a year from the day we met. The day was intimate and simple – perfect! The years that followed would bring us three children and see us travel the world. We would have laughter, tears and headaches but never boredom. A marriage without upset is a marriage without passion, and we love each other still -with a passion. Blue Cloud puffs out his chest to this day, priding himself on his success in bringing us together.

The early days living with a psychic must have been strange for my young wife. I remember her waking me in the night because she could feel the weight of someone in spirit sitting on the bed. When I responded, "Yes, me too." Without opening my eyes. She was not impressed.

"Who is it?" She was shaking me now, more perturbed by the unknown identity of our visitor than his presence.

"I don't know! I'm asleep!" I snapped.

Reluctantly she snuggled back down, leaving one eye open and pulling the covers up to her chin. In time she came to realise that spirit don't always appreciate my need to eat, sleep or in any way live a normal life, and that I need to be firm with them sometimes. In these moments I choose to ignore spirit, not that this stops them, but I have to make time for my own life.

As weeks and months passed, Jane began to accept these events as the norm and soon got into step with this strange new reality. The phrase, 'love me love my dog' springs to mind, although it was more of a 'love me love my ghosts' situation. Before long, wardrobe doors opening on their own or knives and forks rattling in drawers no longer took her by surprise. She realised there was no need to be afraid. It was usually only Pepe in any case.

The first time she spoke to Blue Cloud was without my knowledge. He decided to introduce himself to her one evening as I had been slow to comply with his request. I was seated at my desk when he ambushed me. Jane later told me she heard a strange, booming voice coming out of the office. She slowly peered around the door to find that BC had occupied my body, enabling him to speak with her directly. She slipped quietly in and sat in the seat opposite, usually reserved for clients. His control in those days was not as precise as it came to be, and Jane had to remove the cigarette I had been smoking from my fingers before it burned my hand.

His fractured vocabulary was at times difficult to decipher, but she managed to grasp his meaning, and over the course of many subsequent moonlight chats they developed an unusual rapport. Jane took to recording their meetings so that I could be aware of what he had said. Strangely his tone and the clarity of his voice was not the same as when I heard it directly. Perhaps the necessity of using my vocal chords or something in the mechanics of occupying someone else's body played its part in the transformation. In any case, it was apparent that Jane was adapting well to her unconventional new life. She accepted Blue Cloud as one of the family, as he accepted her.

Luckily Jane came to me already possessing a faith in God and some vague acceptance of an afterlife, so my lifestyle was not too much of a stretch for her. Her grandmother was known to hear two inexplicable knocks when a family member was about to die and often dreamt she was at a family gathering where the person who was about to pass away was absent. Her mum had occasional experiences too. She heard the voice of her dead mother-in-law as they travelled to her funeral. She chatted away in her ear, consoling her that at least she had got a new outfit out of the job. At one point, when a van cut between the hearse and the car they were riding in, she even heard her laugh out loud, shouting, "Watch out, it will be your turn next!". The unmistakable broad Lancashire accent rang out in her ears and the day seemed less daunting for it, although the other mourners probably thought her smiles in the funeral car rather inappropriate.

Jane had been reared on family stories such as these and as such was not fazed by the concept that the dead can communicate. Perhaps this was intended as a kind of preparation for when we found each other, after all, not everyone would be comfortable with this peculiar situation. With hindsight, I suspect Blue Cloud had been paving the way for our paths to cross for years. As a young girl, Jane would have a recurring dream that a giant of a man came looking for her, to carry her away to an unknown place. She would hide behind an armchair, terrified. A clock chimed his arrival and would strike again when it was time for him to leave. These dreams went on for years until one evening he found her, and she realised that he was a kind soul after all, and she need not have been afraid all these years. He lifted her over his head and carried her through vibrant green fields towards the place where she felt she was supposed to be. Jane is sure now that this was Blue Cloud preparing for the right time to bring us together.

Not all dreams mean something. Some are the product of an active mind or a fevered brow. Others are manifestations of our hopes or our fears, but then there are those which convey messages from spirit in picture form, sent down the silver cord like a television signal. We need to interpret what these images mean if we are to understand fully what spirit is trying to tell us. Recurring dreams usually indicate we are being told something important but have not identified what it is. We continue to have them until we have successfully deciphered the meaning. Astral travel within or own dimension or another makes up the final category in the age-old pursuit of the meaning of dreams. Another interesting detail is that it is when we are drifting off to sleep or awakening that we are most susceptible to spiritual influences.

Although I missed my Welsh cottage, our Blackpool home was always full of love and laughter. I realised this was an opportunity to reach a different catchment of people who were perhaps afraid of death, or simply living life like their actions had no consequence. If I was to help people, they needed to know I was here, so I approached the local papers, who duly obliged with the headline, 'I have no hotline to heaven'. This was drawn from my explanation that although I could communicate with those in spirit, I could not click my fingers and summon anyone up. This article did the trick by mentioning I had moved to the area and soon the phone was ringing.

One of the first people to visit me in Blackpool for a reading was a well presented, elderly lady who introduced herself as Mrs Illingworth. She took her seat opposite mine, and I placed my tape recorder on the table between us. I often worked in this way, giving the sitter a cassette to take home so that they could refer to it at their leisure. Straight away a man drew close. His breathing was laboured. As the connection strengthened I heard his name. Doug. Mrs Illingworth confirmed that her late husband, Doug, died from a chest condition four years ago. The next word I heard confused me. He kept repeating, 'moo'. His wife explained with a smile that her name was Muriel, and Doug used to call her Moo. She recognised the large dog he brought with him, and explained that the reason he was rambling on about drains was that she was having problems with the sewers at their home and workmen had been called.

She went home happy, thrilled to have been in touch with Doug. The next day she telephoned, asking to come and see me again as she had something interesting to show me. She arrived clutching the cassette tape. When we played it back, Doug's heavy breathing was clearly audible as Mrs Illingworth and I chatted away.

Around this time, a lady called Mrs Adams from the West Midlands was desperate to see me, but too frail to make the journey. I suggested a postal reading, so she sent me a recent photograph of herself for me to hold. This turned out to be unlike any postal reading I had ever done. My letter began,

Dear Mrs Adams,

I will do what I can for you, although cannot promise anything. I will tune in to spirit and see what I can pick up.

I hope you are keeping cheerful, I have been in spirit for one year today, so you could say this is my first birthday. I have been with you very often over the last twelve months and I have seen you have not been very happy. I have also noticed that you have neglected my house plants. They are all dying! You do realise that this is Charles talking to you? I welcome this opportunity to speak to you once again...

The letter went on to talk about his passing, how much he loved her and what had happened to him. As I read the letter back I was amazed. This had never happened before. I posted it the next day. Mrs Adams was overjoyed to hear from her husband, Charles.

A spiritualist church in nearby Fleetwood asked me to speak to their congregation, and I obliged with pleasure on several occasions, but I came to realise that my real passion lay in going out to reach those who would not dream of ever going to a church. There was a sense of satisfaction in reaching people like that, much more so than preaching to the converted. Jane helped me to get organised and supported me as I held regular demonstrations of clairvoyance at several Blackpool venues, including the North Pier. On one occasion four seaside palm readers came to see me on stage but ironically turned up a day early. The box office saw the funny side and couldn't wait to tell me the next day.

I don't usually remember the messages I give, but one I passed on at Blackpool North Pier has always stuck in my mind. I came to a gentleman standing at the back of the theatre with a man in spirit who had died in the Zeebrugge disaster. The car ferry, 'Herald of Free Enterprise', left Belgium for Dover in March 1987, with bow doors open, causing her to capsize. 193 people perished. This man showed me a huge steering wheel and explained he was a lorry driver, and that he shouldn't have been on the ferry at all. He was standing in that day for a colleague who was sick. He wanted to stress that he was ok now. As the burly man at the back responded to me, I realised he was crying. He was the man who had called in sick.

People flooded to see me for healing and readings and, perhaps too often, I felt sorry for them and didn't charge. I am sure this was the right thing to do, but at times we struggled financially, especially so as by this time Jane was expecting a baby with all the extra expense that it entails.

For the first time in my adult life I was worried about money.

I remember one very elderly lady with crippling arthritis who came to see me one morning for help. Her grey eyes looked so weary and tired of life that I hadn't the heart to charge her. She carefully took a seat, and I placed my hands first upon her head and then onto her gnarled hands. As I did so she looked directly up at me with such pleading eyes and asked if she would soon be pain-free. As the words left her lips, I saw deep blue velvet curtains closing behind her head, a sign that someone is about to pass over. I returned her look and took a second or two to word my answer. "Believe me, before too long you will be free of any pain." She gave me a knowing smile and thanked me. I like to think she knew what I was saying. She passed away just two weeks later.

Around this time, the daughter of a very close friend of mine telephoned to ask for some confidential advice. She was seventeen years old and just out of college. I told her to call round and that there would be no charge. When she arrived, I could see she was upset, but I didn't immediately pick up why. She was pregnant - by an older, married man. Her parents would be devastated, and her career plans were in shreds. She cried and cried, and I shed a tear or two myself, both for her and her father. She told me she had never believed in abortion and had heard horrific stories of vacuums and tiny broken bodies, but now, thrust into this life changing circumstance, she was shocked to find herself considering it. She wanted me to tell her what I knew, from the point of view of spirit, before she decided.

The responsibility of telling her the truth of what I knew so that she could make an informed decision weighed heavily on me. First, I explained how the spirit enters the body soon after conception, and that aborted babies go on to grow to maturity in the spirit world, usually well cared for by extended family members. I told her that they are brought from time to time to see their earthly family and are eventually reunited with them when their parents pass over.

After a hug and a tearful goodbye, she made her way home with food for thought. I lay awake that night, my heart aching for this young girl and her torment. I was hugely sympathetic to her predicament, and I prayed she would make the right decision. I have seen many people who are tormented by remorse after having an abortion, but I never met anyone who said they regret choosing to keep their baby. Even a victim of rape once told me that she wished she had considered having her baby adopted instead of aborting her. She suffered first at the hands of her rapist and again with the guilt, which continually haunted her. Sometimes in life, we are presented with unwanted and undeserved situations. All things for a purpose. If a person discovered a baby on their doorstep, they wouldn't put it in the bin; they would find someone who would care for it if they were unable to do so. Perhaps if more people considered adoption, then many sad, childless couples who are waiting and praying would get their dearest wish.

Some people take the difficult decision to abort a physically disabled or Down's syndrome child and it is so sad. Raising a child with Down's is challenging, but it is also very rewarding. I believe that we can learn a lot from these people.

When I first moved to Wales, I became a member of Toc H, an international Christian charity movement which began as a soldiers club in Belgium during World War I. The purpose of the society is to ease the burden of others through acts of service.

A request went out to the members for volunteers to help with a Special Olympics-type event being held at the Eirias Park Sports Stadium in Colwyn Bay. I was to help supervise the 500-metre race for a group of children and young adults who were mentally challenged. One race, in particular, I will never forget. Eight excited teenage girls, mostly with Down's, lined up to compete. The pistol fired and off they went. One girl was way out in front from the beginning. The crowd were cheering, and she smiled and waved as she ran. When she was around fifty meters from the finishing tape, a gasp went up. The girl who was in second place, although still some distance behind, tripped and fell. The young lady out in front looked around, and when she saw her friend crying on the floor, she stopped and ran back to help her. The other kids raced passed them and crossed the finish line. The crowd went wild as the two girls embraced and hobbled arm in arm together to the finish. There wasn't a dry eye in the stadium. Children with Down's are very spiritual, and they are valued members of the community. We could learn a lot from them.

The next morning I awoke from a broken sleep, still worrying for my friend's daughter. When evening came, she telephoned to say that she had told her parents and that she had decided to have the baby adopted. She seemed focused now the decision was made. When she had the baby, it would go into foster care for six weeks to allow leeway for the mother to change her mind, before going to the adoptive parents.

When the time came, the baby girl was only with foster parents for two weeks before her mother realised that she wanted to keep her after all. She tells me she never regretted her final decision.

Although my work was immensely rewarding, finances remained tight. One evening after a couple of beers I had a fantastic idea that would solve all our financial problems! They call Blackpool the Las Vegas of the North, and sure enough just down the road from where we were living was a casino. Maybe I could use my gift to win just enough money to pay the bills. It had to be worth a try. Jane was unimpressed, but I scraped together the total of one hundred and sixty pounds, suited up and set off to save the day.

It was my first time in a casino. I have never been much of a gambler. I purchased my chips and made straight for the roulette wheel like James Bond, if James Bond was really awkward and nervous that is. I sat at the table and watched for a minute or two. Got it! I confidently put some chips on black eight and held my breath as the ball clattered around.

"Red eighteen!" the croupier called out.

I was sure it would be black eight. Baffled at what had gone wrong, I tried again. I placed my chips on red twelve.

"Black eight!" She had to be kidding! The ball was spinning with the wheel now, firmly wedged in the number I had previously chosen.

Undaunted I watched for a moment then placed another bet. Black twenty-two. The ball took forever to settle, and when it did there it was - red twelve! I could hardly believe it. The numbers continued to follow me around the table, the ball repeatedly landing on the one I chose the last time.

I was home, penniless and deflated before midnight, greeted by rolling eyes and I told you so. This was not my finest hour, but the penny had dropped. It was a mistake I would never repeat. Spirit didn't speak to me about it, but I drew the conclusion that they were showing me that my abilities were indeed intact, but I was not going to be allowed to use them in this way. People often ask me to give them the lottery numbers or the winner of the Grand National. When they do, I recount this story to demonstrate that alas, it doesn't quite work like that.

It was only a matter of days later that a pub called Royalles in nearby Lytham telephoned to ask for my help with what they referred to as 'spooky goings on'. New landlord Alex and his wife Pat were beginning to regret their move to the pub, a four storey naval themed bar formerly known as the Ship and Royal. Glasses flying off the bar, light bulbs popping and other strange happenings were frightening the couple and their staff, so I agreed to call in one evening and take a look.

Lytham is a charming seaside town, not as uncouth or flamboyant as her sister, Blackpool. I found Royalles taking pride of place on the main street of small shops and boutiques. It was a grand, four-storey, old lady of a building, though neon signs now shone onto the street from its second-floor windows in a bid to drag it kicking and screaming into the twentieth century.

The interior had been modernised into a large, open-plan space, and as I entered the pub, the landlord was engaging his customers in some friendly Glaswegian banter. I bought a pint, introduced myself and he welcomed me enthusiastically. I found Alex to be a pleasant, solid built, bearded man, both younger and taller than I had expected. I could not imagine this giant Scotsman being afraid of anything. His wife joined us at a table, and I asked them to describe what had been happening.

It began, Pat explained, with the bangs, creaks and moans. Then one afternoon as she was having coffee with friends, something moved her chair – with her in it! On another occasion, money from the tills had gone missing from her cash bag. At first, she did not suspect anything ghostly, but then it re-appeared one night in a disused upstairs room, laid out on the carpet in a perfect circle. Events were gathering momentum and the couple just wanted some peace restoring to their hectic lifestyles.

By the time they had finished their stories the downstairs bar was busy, so I asked if I could start by taking a look upstairs. A wide staircase turned and took us up to the first-floor landing. The décor was faded but had obviously been quite lavish in its day. Double doors on the right took us through into what looked in the dark like a vast, disused function room. As the switch was clicked only one light engaged.

"This was the figurehead bar," Alex whispered as if trying not to wake them.

From the walls of the cedar-scented room, large cobwebbed faces leant over us in the half-light, scrutinising the uninvited guests from their musty resting places. The ship's figureheads gave dubious character to the room. As I took in the chisel furrowed brows and muted blues and reds of their wooden clothing, a man began to take shape in the shadows. He looked around sixty, with silver hair and a waxed handlebar moustache. On his chest, a flamboyant burgundy waistcoat glistened with gold embroidery. He was holding a whisky glass, and a sudden movement at his feet drew my attention to the black and white collie that nestled there.

"William," he said with a nod, "but you can call me Charlie."

I indicated the place where he stood and asked Alex if he could see anything. As his eyes became accustomed to the dark, he reported seeing a shapeless mist which moved across the room to the window as we spoke.

It transpired that Charlie was quite a character. He had been a regular in the figurehead bar until his death in a plane crash, after which he 'woke up dead' and returned to his favourite 'haunt' so to speak. He mentioned someone called Sarah, but I was unclear who she was.

Alex and Pat were relieved that the source of the disturbances was just an old man hankering after a lock in and not the demonic force they had feared. As we went downstairs, I explained that he was happy enough, although somewhat reluctant to leave. After a short conversation where I assured them that, having made his presence felt the activity would probably subside, they decided to let him stay.

That night in bed I was telling Jane about Charlie when I had an idea. The disused figurehead bar had such a fantastic atmosphere, it would make an ideal venue for a kind of Psychic Club. I could hold public demonstrations of clairvoyance, have guest speakers and even have a development circle there for anyone interested in nurturing their psychic ability. Everyone has the capacity to be psychic to some degree, a spark that can be fanned into a flame. There is a knock at the door, and you instinctively know who it is, you think of a long lost relative and out of the blue they call, you dream something that comes true or perhaps just for a second catch a glimpse of someone out of the corner of your eye. With guidance, you can develop this, and it is true that we never stop developing, but it must come from the heart. Before one becomes a practising medium, there is a lot to learn. When practised professionally or otherwise, mediumship should be regarded as a most honourable and indeed dedicated way of life. Meditate on love, absorb love, give love and become alight with the divine fire to heal the sick, comfort the bereaved and bring peace. In a psychic development circle, one can safely learn. It is the only safe way, as experimenting outside the protection of a circle can be dangerous. An accomplished medium must always head the circle to ensure the safety of the group, and their guide takes control of the corresponding circle in spirit. The best results are achieved by maintaining regular sitting times when all minds are agreeable and in harmony with each other. This atmosphere is helped along by beginning the circle with a prayer and perhaps a short talk so that all are on the same wavelength.

The word 'séance' simply means a 'sitting'. It is the sitting together of a group of people in a psychic experiment. These sessions tend to be more successful when held in the evening. In theory, you can conduct one at any time, but in practice, there is a stillness in the night time which is absent during the day. Low lighting and soft music add to the atmosphere and aids relaxation. The figurehead bar would be the perfect setting to hold a regular development circle. The following day I took Jane to see the room and booked it indefinitely for every Thursday evening.

The night of the launch came, and I nervously nursed a pint as Jane set out fifty chairs upstairs. I had put up a few posters, placed a couple of ads in the local paper and was hoping that people would turn up. As eight o'clock approached I drained my glass and slowly climbed the once-grand staircase to the dusty figurehead bar. A large group of people stood outside the double doors at the top of the stairs, spilling onto the top steps. The ones at the front were in conversation with Jane. Standing on the top stair, I fed my hand and arm into a gap, led with my shoulder and tried to squeeze through the crowd. A large lady spun her head around, looking over her shoulder to glare at me, nose to nose.

"Excuse me." I simpered.

"It's full. You can't get in. You'll have to come back next week like us."

Jane overheard the confrontation and tried to diffuse the situation with a joke. "If *he* doesn't get in there won't *be* an evening of clairvoyance!"

I breached the barricade and opened the door, but had a similar problem getting through to the front. Extra chairs had been squeezed in, and people were standing at the back and down the sides of the room, which began to quieten as I fought my way to my post. As I surveyed the crowd, two things sprang to mind. Firstly, as Jane peered at me through the glass doors, unable to fit inside, we were probably breaching fire regulations, and secondly, it struck me just how much interest there is in the subject. People had come from all over the Fylde Coast and the North West. It was encouraging to see how they were searching for something more in this material world, how they were thirsting for knowledge. I was also very aware that most were hoping to receive a message that night, and I would certainly do my best to deliver, but they would not leave before I had also sown a few seeds about becoming more spiritual. Of course, some of my words fell on stony ground, but this message, whilst incidental to them, was far more important in my opinion than the hello from their gran.

Nonetheless, my attention was drawn to a slim lady on the back row, and an older voice in my ear informed me that she was wearing three rings that used to belong to her. The girl nodded in response, and I joked that it was ok, she didn't want them back. The laughter helped the audience to relax, which helps me enormously, and the evening was under way. I also picked up that she had a problem in her stomach area. She responded that her gall bladder had recently been removed. The voice added ominously that the problem wasn't over.

On the front row, a young man in jeans was visited by a gentleman called Bob who had been six feet tall before having both legs amputated. He told me he died from chest problems. "Pneumonia," the young man responded. I explained that Bob was now complete in every way but that he showed himself with his disability so that he could be easily recognised.

In the second half I tried some psychometry, which translates as a 'measure of the soul', but a more accurate definition might be the 'measurement or perception by the intuitive faculties of the spirit.' It is the art of reading the influences of an article by holding it. I say art rather than a gift because it is something you can learn to do. Impressions vary in intensity depending on several factors, including the ability to free the mind of outside interference and the atmosphere which has affected the article. I held objects belonging to members of the audience to see what character, surroundings and influences I could read from them. To finish the evening, I held a question and answer session, which was cut short by the last orders bell sounding from downstairs.

Friday's local rag delighted in the headline, 'Unforeseen success of Psychic club'. I booked guest mediums and organised development circles for the first Thursday of each month. Sometimes Blue Cloud or Pepe would speak to the circle with some wise words to help the sitters. Others from lower planes would seek out the circle to learn. One interesting character called Joey became a regular visitor. If nothing else he showed the group that not everyone who dies has a great understanding. His language could be a little colourful, and he would chat about his long-suffering wife Linda and his time in prison. As he learned a few basic lessons, they reflected in his words, which I have edited of any expletives.

Joey; "When you die you might expect to float on a cloud. You might expect to see angels with wings. The last thing you expect to find is a group of American Indians!

I haven't been over very long. I lived between Dudley and Tipton. I'm quite happy on plane one. I pop back sometimes to visit my old local pub where I used to drink Banks' mild beer. When I go back, they say the place is haunted. I was locked up in prison once. Winson Green. I got a telling off from the judge. You know why I got a telling off? Because I'd done something wrong.

I failed my eleven-plus exam. I did my best though. That's a good answer, isn't it? I said to my old man, 'I tried my best.

You can't do better than that.' You know what he did? He kicked me and walloped me! My mate didn't try at all. Who did best, me or him? I tried hard and got some of the questions right but we both failed.

You might find yourselves over here being questioned, and it's no good saying you tried hard if you failed.

Here you have to learn all the time. There was this man who was a millionaire. He's down there now. He said he'd give a million pounds to get another life, but you can't pay your way out of the pit. He should have thought about that before. It's too late now. He's dead and down there.

My spirit guide is still here. He talks to me sometimes. Shows me things I've got to accept. I'm told things, and I think they must be right, but if I can't accept it, I don't go higher. If it hasn't gone in, I'm not gonna go up. I'm questioning. It's not a bad thing to question, but right is right and wrong is wrong whatever you think.

I think it's good for you people to speak to someone like me who isn't high up. Don't think you lot are any better than me. I'm telling you now, one or two of you are worse!"

When Blue Cloud spoke, it was with authority but also with compassion. He took a genuine interest in the spiritual welfare of the sitters, who came to look forward to his words. Here are some excerpts from the circles, which Jane recorded onto cassette so that I could listen to what he had to say.

BC; *"Good evening my friends. Evening or morning makes no difference to me, but I say 'good evening' because it is evening to you. Each day feel the wind, see the sky, talk to the Almighty One. Feel His presence. Use all senses. Use what you have.*

When I was on the Earth, before we go into battle do you know why we dress? There is a possibility that we die. We knew when we die we go to our friends in spirit, and we stand before the Almighty, and so we dress for this. We prepare, just in case. It is good to prepare yourselves for every eventuality. Remember these words.

We gave with the left hand. The left hand is good – close to the heart. We fought with the right hand. There is good and bad in all people. Squash the bad, cultivate the good. We give you opportunities to go higher. It is good! The goal throughout the earthly life is to go high. BC pray to the Almighty One that if it is ever possible for you, His children, to go high, then this will be good.

I was born in what you call Canada, south of Lake Winnipeg. I passed over in 1647. I lived to be 124! I learned my English from a man who was French. I lived a good life then walked up the mountain when it was time to go. I was very tall man in charge of many people, chief, therefore least important person. We were very happy people, although you may call 'hard times'. My boy replaced me in charge when he was 75 years old. My grandson was then 50.

When I walked the land, I walked many, many miles in the presence always of the Almighty. I asked the Great Spirit to guide me. How can life be hard when you walk with Him? Life is hard when you walk away from Him. How could I go the wrong way? Every week I sing, dance, talk with Him. I gave thanks to Him for all that I had. If I worry about anything, I told Him of my worry. The rest of the tribe they come to me and ask me many questions – wise man! I say, 'I hear your words. Tomorrow I give you answer.' They know I give them answer because I wise man. I know first I must ask Him the question, and I sleep. In my sleep, I travel, and He gives me the answer. So the following day I see all the leaders of the tribes, and I give them the answers – BC wise man! But not BC wise man – only wise enough to ask Him!"

"We from high spirit speak to you at all times. Our words from our minds enter your subconscious mind. You then have to reach into your subconscious and drag them out. We can ask of you or suggest to you. Beware, sometimes low spirit can enter your subconscious. You must throw out!

Do not say, 'What do spirit think?' There are many, many people in spirit, and we do not all think the same, do you understand?

Now my friends and my family, listen very carefully to the words of a wise old man. Each day watch every thought in your head. Each time you have a thought, is it from high spirit, low spirit or yourselves? Watch every word. Only speak if you have something to say. Watch who you are speaking to and think carefully before you speak. If you have doubt, do not speak. Guard your footsteps, guard your thoughts, watch carefully your words. Each night spirit try to talk to you. Sometimes we get through, sometimes not. Ideas can be put into your head. Ideas for you to think over. We do not always say, 'This is what you must do'. We expect you to use your own mind.

Listen to my words. Time on the earth is precious. Do not collect rubbish. Listen and accept what is good. Speak clearly.

You astral project many times, sometimes you remember, sometimes not but we take you and show you many times. We can take you to visit – maybe your granddad. From time to time we will show you the way, and we will show you where you go when you depart this world. When you depart, you will go toward the light. If, heaven forbid, you depart this world and find yourself in the dark, and you see a light, go to the light and you will be helped over.

Each day, pray to the Almighty One because you are like little children with the loving Father. At the end of the day He wishes to listen to you and speak to you."

"A little child has an enormous box of chocolates and sits in the corner eating. The parent will say, 'No more,' and take away from the child. The child will say, 'Why do they do this to me?' Mamma and Papa do this for the child's sake. If the child took the chocolates and gave them to the other boys and girls who do not have any, the parent would not remove. Understand the Almighty One as much as you can, because the loving parent knows when to remove and when to let you have.

Understand two words tonight, 'unselfish' and 'motive'. Try to be unselfish. The motive behind what you do is very important."

It was around this time that another of my helpers made himself known and occasionally spoke through me in circle to the group. He had a swarthy complexion, long, black hair, a beard and dark, deep-set eyes. His clothing consisted of robes that appeared to be made of sacking, and he introduced himself as Bart.

Bart was more matter of fact than my other helpers and had no time to waste on tact. He would indicate which direction to go, and he came with love, but if anyone chose to ignore his advice he had no interest in coaxing them back to the right path. They had been given their chance. Like a signpost, he would point the way but was disinterested if you got lost. He had done his job, and that was that. In circle, his voice was soft but bore the authority of high spirit. The group sensed this and were in awe of him when he came through. He would sway back and forth in a nodding motion, palms together as he said what he came to say, then he would offer a blessing and leave without ceremony.

Bart; *"Peace be with you. When we speak to you, it is our spirit which speaks. This is more difficult than you understand. You may speak with me. I speak the truth."*

"We are here to overlook the plan and to see it carried through. I never intended a life on Earth. I look at the plan from where we are. We decide where to go from here."

"The world is an untidy place. Much work to do.

We here from the highest of spirit stand on the door for the Almighty One, to welcome those who deserve to come here. There is one who stands on a door down in the pits. He is busier than I. He has more visitors. There are many with me and many with him. We try to influence; they try to influence."

At one meeting I told Karen, a regular sitter, that she should see a doctor as I could see her gallbladder was full of stones. She had it checked out, and the hospital confirmed that this was indeed the case. The consultant arranged for her to have the gallbladder removed and in the meantime, Karen had three spiritual healing sessions. The day after the operation the surgeon visited her bedside, flabbergasted that they had only found three stones. The rest had disappeared.

I was proud when regular sitters began to see and hear things for themselves, but even more so when I noticed after a few months that they seemed to be becoming more spiritual. We always made time for spiritual philosophy, and the group embraced this as enthusiastically as the contact with spirit. It is far more important to be spiritual than psychic, and to be psychic without being spiritual is a recipe for disaster. They started to think about their actions more and became increasingly compassionate and helpful to each other. Personalities began to cast off their ego and gain a whole new perspective. It was a delight to see. Members travelled in all weathers from as far afield as Preston and the Lake District. We became a community, old ladies, lorry drivers, young couples and even a circus ringmaster, but we always welcomed new visitors and members wholeheartedly. I had seen some spiritualist churches become cliquey and I was very careful not to go down that road. I remember the Lytham Psychic Club with so much affection now. It was to run and run for many years, all thanks to Charlie and his mischief.

I carried on with my evenings of clairvoyance around the country, this week Birmingham, the next week Hull, but I returned to home territory and the Psychic Club every Thursday. By now we had two little girls, Ayesha and Sian. Jane's mother would babysit so that she could come with me and help with taking tickets and managing my diary. I delighted in being a dad, and the girls grew up with spirit like it was the most natural thing in the world. This was a refreshing way to live in contrast to my childhood, although there was some confusion at nursery when Ayesha's response to being asked what she would like to be when she grew up was either a spirit guide or a duck.

I fitted in appointments for private readings or healing as and when I was home. One summer's afternoon in the middle of a busy day I opened the door to a professional lady. The entry in my appointment diary read simply 'Maureen'. Although she was diminutive in stature, here was a person who was quite obviously a force of nature. The cropped red hair suited her energetic personality, and a warm, broad smile never seemed to leave her lips. As she sat before me, the blue in her aura, which I explained changes hourly, perfectly matched her flowing denim skirt suit and shoulder padded jacket. A small lady in spirit stood behind her. She gesticulated but didn't speak to me. Maureen's mother had been profoundly deaf in life. I explained that she no longer had this disability, but showed herself this way for recognition purposes. It is a common practice when spirit try to communicate, that they appear in such a way that they will be known to their loved one.

A friend of Maureen's had previously seen me at a venue in Preston, and was initially unimpressed by three life changing events I had predicted. They made absolutely no sense to her at the time, and she had walked away feeling disappointed. Two weeks later however, these happenings, which included a surprise pregnancy, a career move and foreign travel at short notice, had all fallen dramatically into place. Her recommendation led Maureen to come to see me for a reading, who was equally impressed by the messages she received.

When Maureen discovered that I also did healing, she confided in me that she was suffering from second stage diverticulitis. Harley Street doctors had referred her for tests in London's Portland Street Hospital, where they wanted to perform a colostomy due to severe inflammation and the risk of a perforated bowel. She wanted to avoid this at all costs and asked for my help.

Turning to leave that day, she hesitated and informed me that she had some experience in promotions and thought that I could help so many people if I only had the right exposure. I thanked her for her comments, and we said goodbye. Several weeks later she appeared at our door again, this time with a bottle of champagne, a tray of eggs from her husband's egg farm and a promise to help me reach more people. She had returned to her doctor, who informed her that her most recent x-ray was clear, and there was no need to operate. It was strange to think that a series of coincidences and chance meetings led this lady to my door, and even stranger that she had experience in promotions and an enthusiastic desire to help spread the word. It was as though spirit were putting things into place.

True to her word, Maureen helped me from that day onwards. She publicised events as well as helping out generally with whatever was needed. She and her son Mark, who soon came to take an equal interest in my work, were soon to become close and long lasting family friends.

It was around this time that a blonde young man in jeans also came to see me for a reading. When we were finished, he introduced himself in his Yorkshire twang as Ian Calvert, Disc Jockey with Red Rose Radio in Preston.

He had heard some people talking about me and after the sitting admitted that he had wanted to see for himself if I was any good. He explained he was a night-time presenter who started life as a radio station tea boy and went on to impress with his music expertise. He invited me to appear with him every Thursday evening on a phone in programme especially dedicated to psychic phenomena and the work I do. It was a welcome opportunity, and the timing was perfect. After I had left the Psychic Club, there was just enough time to drive to the studio before the programme began.

The show ran and ran. One call I remember quite vividly because it highlighted the misconceptions that too often go unspoken. An obviously intellectual young man named Darren, who had been having a discussion with friends, asked me to settle a disagreement. Pop culture, he told me, says that hell is where the devil punishes you for all time, but if you are doing what the devil wants by being bad, why would he punish you? Was this anomaly proof that the devil doesn't exist? The devil is happy for people to disbelieve his existence. That way no one is guarded against him. I hope my answer clarified things for the listeners.

Going to hell is not the punishment of the devil, it is quite simply God's natural laws, which ensure you go where you deserve to be. In fact, quite to the contrary, the devil will often offer you sweeteners to tempt you to follow in his ways. If you ignore the needs of others and are selfish, you may well accumulate all kind of earthly pleasures for yourself. When you pass over, however, you will be the one whose needs are overlooked as you descend to join others who like yourself have done the devil's work, often without even realising. He is not the one punishing you with an existence in hell, although he is happy to have led you there.

It was during these Red Rose Radio shows that I predicted the political downfall of Margaret Thatcher, and while the world's attention was focused on potential problems between the US and USSR, predicted that a Middle East crisis ahead would be the most critical issue.

I was amused when Ian told me he was always a little spooked when I went home and left him alone in the shadowy building in the early hours of the morning after my slot was over. The studios were housed in a disused church, and he would listen for every noise in case I had left any spirits behind. Similarly, when I visited a person's home to give a reading, they would often thank me as I left, before politely asking if I could take all the spirits away with me. This always made me smile. People often don't understand that those in spirit were there with them regardless of my presence. I don't conjure anyone up.

1
Being David

1988 was a year of change. The Soviets withdrew from Afghanistan, the Iran-Iraqi war ended, Pope John Paul II addressed the European Parliament (while Ian Paisley heckled and denounced him as the antichrist), and the first murder conviction based on DNA evidence took place in the UK. It was a year of change for me too. A storm was coming.

Home life was perfect. We were content in our small flat, living simply but with everything we needed. The oven didn't work; the bedroom was freezing, and the lock on the bathroom delighted in holding us captive from time to time, but we had all we needed to keep us content. Having two little ones did not stop Jane and me from laughing and loving like children ourselves. We worked and played hard, resting only when necessity demanded. I was happy with my Jane, and the thought of change unsettled me. It disturbed me because I knew it was coming, and I knew I was helpless to resist it. It was in the very air I was breathing.

The metamorphosis, when it came, happened in stages. Blue Cloud stood by the fireplace one cold, winter's afternoon and cryptically announced that the time was coming. He was not specific, but his words unnerved me. They hung like a sword over my head. He would wait just long enough for me to forget he ever spoke, before appearing again to reiterate the phrase, or sometimes he would just give me that look that said it all. In a mark of defiance, I elected to avoid eye contact and directed my thoughts to him.

"Just leave me alone."

His reply was cryptic and ambiguous. "Who are you fighting? Only yourself!"

As weeks passed, a new, oppressive sensation seized me which slowly grew in intensity, like a million people in spirit leaning on my back. I have never been more tempted to turn my back on my gifts and just be whatever I wanted. Why shouldn't I just live a normal life like everyone else?

In those days of early transformation, strange experiences engulfed me. While I slept, and even when awake and daydreaming I would see myself as someone else - recall memories that weren't mine. These episodes would feature people I knew and yet didn't know, events I remembered that I had not experienced. It was as though I was walking through Marks & Spencer's trying on different outfits. David Drew was just one of the garments. A voice I didn't recognise whispered softly in my ear one morning, "You have walked the earth many times and worn many guises."

I tried to shake the intrusive thoughts. What was wrong with me? I was desperate to hang on to my old self, but with each passing day my identity was slipping away, and I was afraid.

Jane was visibly concerned by my altered mood. She repeatedly asked if I was alright - if I was worried about something. I didn't mean to be evasive; we told each other everything, but how could I explain to her what I didn't understand myself? I know she tried to support me, to comfort me, but she was fumbling blind. The distractions of daily life helped me at first, but soon just going shopping or taking the girls to the park couldn't block out the howling winds of change that were threatening to take me.

My granddad was a miner. When he walked to the colliery to begin a shift down the pit, he would take his time, appreciating his surroundings along the way. He would study the shape of the clouds and the shadow of trees, smell the cut grass and relish the breeze against his cheeks before it was time to climb into the blackened lift and leave the sunlight behind. I thought of him often as I savoured each day in just the same way. Despite my protestations Blue Cloud was right. I knew a time was coming, but for what?

Realisations unfurled before me daily, like fog dispersing to reveal an unexpected path. We are born to this life, then a time comes when we are born to the next on one of the unseen spirit planes. From there we learn and progress, perhaps having another earthly life, forgetting our former personality. When we reach the fourth level in the spirit world, we begin to remember our past lives on Earth as well as our other existences in spirit. The mind, which is part of our real, immortal self, opens up, allowing us access to the chambers where information about our previous existences is stored. At this point we evolve into a kind of accumulation of all the people we ever were, with the collective knowledge we gained throughout all of those lives. That is not to say that we cease to be the person we are, just that there becomes more to us than that. If you think back to the baby, the child and the teen you once were, are you not still that person despite being very different now? Are ice, water and steam not the same in essence despite being solid, liquid and vapour?

This state of becoming the accumulation of all we ever were only happens when we are in the spirit world. While alive the biggest insight the average person may get into their former lives is a dream, a sense of déjà vu or perhaps the feeling that they recognise someone they have never met.

All people walking the earth have a symbolic thermometer on their back, which goes up and down to denote their level of spirituality, that is to say, the plane they would go to if they died at that very moment. Even those who would be on level four will not become the accumulation whilst on the earth. We come here with a clean sheet, and in any case, the infinite is impossible to truly absorb while we are contained in these finite surroundings. For the duration of this life it is deemed better not to know.

It came as a huge shock therefore when Bart revealed to me that I was sent here with the specific intention of becoming the accumulation while living my earthly life. This unheard of situation was apparently due to the course my life was meant to take. Those on the high spirit planes were expressing the hope that I would take up the gauntlet and use my life as was always intended, to help people understand, not just that there is life after death, but more importantly that the way they live their life, crucially affects their destination and ultimately their spiritual progression. When I learned that over 60% of people who passed over were going straight to the pits, it drove home the urgency of the situation. My life was a rescue mission, and to succeed I would need all the knowledge that lay dormant in my higher self, a kind of 'download' from my 'spiritual iCloud', as it were.

Blue Cloud told me not to be afraid. "You are not losing a part, but gaining the whole. You see me as my last incarnation, but am I not also the accumulation?"

I understood the importance of this plan, which was laid down long before I was born. Of course, I did. I also knew what a unique circumstance this was, but the enormity of the situation weighed heavily on me, and I was terrified of losing my identity.

This new information did at least make sense of my strange childhood, why I had to be different, but still I didn't want it to be true. I was desperate to cling on to who I was. I felt like I was running down an upward moving escalator, too afraid to glance behind me. High spirit spoke as though this was a gift, but to me it was a yoke on my shoulders - a tremendous responsibility. What if I didn't like the new me? What if Jane didn't?

Each day as the enormity of my situation was revealed, I thought I would go crazy. I stared across at Jane one evening as she watched some mundane soap on TV and I wondered if she would still love me after this transformation took place. It was a change she hadn't bargained on – I hadn't bargained on, and I didn't want to ruin our life together. As a million thoughts passed behind my eyes, she noticed my expression and crossed the room to hold me. Settling on the chair arm, she kissed me on the head.

"Are you ok?"

This small sympathetic act from the person I had unwittingly dragged into this situation was the last thing I needed. Fighting tears I stood up, shaking loose from her embrace. If I didn't have a family this would not be half so hard - yet without them beside me I feared I wouldn't succeed. It was all so confusing.

"I have to go away for a few days." The words sounded unintentionally cold, tense.

I needed time to meditate. I wanted to protect my girls from whatever was happening. I paced the floor, not quite knowing what to do with myself or how to process my feelings.

That weekend I threw a few things in a bag and assured Jane I would be home soon, that I just needed to get my head together, then I kissed her as though it was our last goodbye. She took my face in her hands and told me that everything would be alright, and she would be saying big prayers for me. I jumped in the car and headed for the heart of Snowdonia.

The three days I spent walking in the wild beauty of the Welsh mountains are a blur to me now. I meditated, prayed and started to become the man I would be for the rest of my life.

When you pray correctly you converse with God, and He always answers, although not always in the way you might imagine, nor necessarily with the hoped for response. If my little girls asked me for a motorbike, the answer would be no. Parents know what their children are ready for and what is good for them. God knows what we need better than we do. If we remember to ask Him, He will make sure we have all we need and more. Quite naturally we think as men think, not as God thinks, but nonetheless, prayer is a very real power.

In 2012 Bolton Wanderers and Tottenham Hotspur were playing in the quarter final of an F. A. Cup match. In the first half, in full view of a stadium full of people and millions of TV viewers at home, Bolton player Fabrice Muamba suffered a cardiac arrest. He lay on the pitch, medics defibrillated him and the world held their breath. Many of the spectators were crying, and they prayed. His heart stopped for 78 minutes, and it was thought all hope was lost, Muamba went on to make a full recovery against all the odds. His consultant said his recovery exceeded their expectations, and Muamba made a retirement statement in which he thanked God he was alive. All those people praying at the same time. He had more help than perhaps he knows.

Everyone should pray at least twice daily, once for the key and once for the bolt. My morning prayer is the key. It invites God into my day as I ask that He is with me, helping me to do the right thing and to see all opportunities to do His will. The evening prayer is the bolt. I ask for protection through the night and a blessing on my home and family. There are many ways to pray. At the Wailing Wall in Jerusalem, the most Holy site of Israel, prayers on tiny rolls of paper are pushed into the cracks. At St. Hywyn's Church in Aberdaron North Wales, prayers are written on stones from the beach and left in a pile on the flagstone floor. All that is needed to pray effectively is to meditate deeply and uninterrupted. In the quietness, you can be at one with God. A prayer from the heart is mightier than a prayer from the lips which is recited verbatim without thought. How many people kneel in church and chant The Lord's Prayer or the 23rd Psalm without understanding what they are saying? This is not prayer.

Inspiration enveloped me that weekend on the mountain. How can anyone look up at the stars and not believe in God? I remembered with some clarity who I had been in other lives and the details of my existences in the spirit world. No one dies and goes straight to heaven. Death does not turn a sinner into a saint or a fool into a wise man. We have to earn our progression through many vastly varying levels.

I recalled level one being similar to the earth. The people here tend to think on a material rather than spiritual level and for this reason, they live in houses and wear clothes. These are all created with the power of their thought, which also enables them to travel great distances in a fraction of a second. At first they may perceive they still have earthly needs – hunger, thirst or other inclinations. Eventually they come to realise that they are not of the material world and no longer need these things.

Animals also have an afterlife, although they are not on a pathway of progression as we are and are therefore often reincarnated very quickly. I have often seen dogs with people at my meetings and on one occasion even a horse who had been put to sleep one week before the meeting. When you pass to this first plane, a departed pet can be with you if you wish it. Auras tend to be cloudy here, however, due to poor understanding, giving this realm a greyish hue.

Each higher plane is a more spiritual place than the last. Level two is also quite similar to the earth, but there is a feel of bright sunshine and beautiful countryside rather than an inner city atmosphere. No grey auras here. Most people have lost their physical desires and are beginning to realise their mistakes and learn from them.

On level three, earthly clothing is no longer necessary, and people are adorned in robes of coloured light. From this level upwards there is no need for speech as communication is made telepathically. There are no language barriers here. You may pass through halls of learning where you inwardly digest new information. People spend extended periods of time in prayer and receive teaching from those who are higher.

It is on the fourth plane that people begin to remember their past lives and recall their previous spiritual knowledge. Their auras radiate all the colours of the rainbow. From here they may travel down to help those dwelling on planes one, two and three, but they are not yet sufficiently developed to be able to visit the pits without being in danger of getting sucked in. Here they receive in-depth teaching from those above, who travel down to teach, speaking to them in simplified terms in the hope that they will be better understood. Each point they explain raises further questions, and the more people learn, the more they realise how little they know.

Like a playground slide, it is always easier to slip down than to climb up. Although those higher can travel down to teach or visit those below, from lower spirit planes they cannot visit higher realms unless taken there to visit under special circumstances. If they want to go high, they must earn their progression. Where husband and wife go to different planes upon passing, the higher can visit the lower, or may even hold back their development to stay with their partner, but the one who is lower cannot travel up to visit.

Once on level five people are far enough advanced to become spirit helpers, but they are not yet wise enough to be a guide to someone on Earth. From here you can safely travel as far down as the pits to try to help others. Those who belong here are completely unselfish and begin to understand God's hidden wisdom.

By the time you reach level six you are highly developed and may be a spirit guide to someone on Earth. To those lower you will appear like a star in the sky. People here speak with authority and will no longer need to have another life on Earth for progression purposes.

Level seven holds beauties you could not imagine and those who dwell here are adorned in bright, radiating colours like the material world has never seen. In your spirituality and love, you will endeavour to influence those who are lower, and they will hang on your every word. You are almost at one with God.

It is impossible to attempt to describe the wonders of Heaven, except to say that here you have reached your goal and are with God's ministering angels, at one with Him. You could not imagine the beauty, the peace and the all-embracing love here.

Just as heaven is being at one with God, hell is being apart from Him, or in other words not being aware of His love for you. You might be surprised by the type of people you find in the dank, grey, miserable realms of the pits. It is not just murderers and the stereotypically evil that end up there, in fact, more people go down to these dismal lands than sail up to the higher, brighter planes. Those who were materialistically minded wander around, their hooded heads bowed low, weighed down by their selfish lives. They have placed their priorities on wealth instead of on helping others. Many amenable but wealthy people end up here, as the more materialistic you are, the less chance you have of developing spiritually. Human desire is like the pits; there is always room for more. Too many people take the 'eat, drink and be merry, life is too short' philosophy, unaware that life is eternal, and their actions have consequence. If you have more than you need while others in the world go without, it will weigh you down. These people may think they will be saved by helping out their friends and family, but even thieves and mobsters help their own. We should seek out need in anyone and help if we can.

Some people from history who might not appear to have led such bad lives dwell down there. Their thoughts, words and deeds are laid bare for all to see. There is no camouflage here, or indeed on any spirit plane. On the earth, you can conceal your real character and fool people into thinking you are something you are not. Those who have not been found out during their life on Earth will be exposed here. Once you pass over you cannot hide, and who you really are is clear for all to see.

The many levels within the pits vary. Nearest the earth are tortured, repentant souls who may one day earn the right to try again with another earthly life. Further into the depths dwell those who prefer to hide in the dark like burglars. Some even aspire to be demons. Progression is open to all who deserve it, but from the pits, you must touch the earth before you can go higher. Alas, some people earn the right to another life but then go on to make the same mistakes over again and can yo-yo between the earth and the pits for centuries. Those who come from this level and go on to be miscarried or stillborn are surprisingly fortunate, as they can have the chance to progress higher by just brushing the earth plane on their journey to the realms above.

We are all playing a game of snakes and ladders. Each time our thoughts and actions toward others demonstrate our love of God we begin to climb a ladder. When we reject God by our selfish actions, we slide down a snake. Where we are when the game ends determines our fate.

If people could take a peep at the horrific existence in the pits, they would immediately change the way they live their lives and save themselves this suffering. The simple way to find happiness in this world and the next is simply to make others happy. If you do all you can to help others, then God will help you. Those who just help themselves do so alone and they will pay the price. It was evident to me now that this was the reason I had been born different, with the gift that I often viewed as a curse, to give people that glimpse of where they are headed and point the way to safety.

Some people mistakenly assume that if they believe in God, it is enough to get them into heaven. It is not. Many think that if they do things in His name they automatically get a ticket to the top. This is not true. Wars and terrorist attacks are frequently made in the name of God as if this pleases Him. When siblings fight in the playground, any parent is naturally disappointed and sad. There is no such thing as a holy war. No matter what you call Him or what road you take to reach Him, the way to love Him is to love all His creations. When you truly love God this becomes your automatic response.

The knowledge I had acquired before this life, came back to me in a kind of osmosis. A change was taking place whether I liked it or not, and as information flooded in I began to understand things better. I put my trust in God and stopped resisting. I found peace in the realisation that when He is with you, there is nothing to fear. We should never question His wisdom. He created all things, the earth, the seas, the wind, the sun and the rain. He alone decided how big the earth would be. He knows all things. Who are we to question Him? As the revelations unfolded, I realised that knowing the purpose for my life would take away the defence that I did not understand. When it was time for me to account for my mistakes there could be no excuses.

Bits and pieces of my memory came together like a picture puzzle taking shape. I remembered being in spirit looking down on the earth like watching a football match from the stands. From the comfort of your seat it is easy to delude yourself that you could do much better. Why don't they pass the ball, why doesn't he shoot? People were making such a mess of their lives before dying, having acquired very little spiritual knowledge.

I remembered the First World War, so much loss as ten million people passed over prematurely over a period of four earthly years. We were kept busy lifting souls from the mud and stench as they were wrenched from one world to another. From spirit, we tried to influence the minds of men, but it is imperative that each person has their own free will, and our words were too often obliterated by the roar of conflict. Lessons were not learned, and soon World War II was upon them, and the carnage began all over again. When it was over, people rebuilt their lives with emphasis on the material rather than the spiritual. Something had to be done. The human race was meandering down a perilous path. Someone needed to come down and act as a signpost, to show people how they should be living if they were to avoid the pits. The learning plane had forgotten its lessons and there was no teacher to help.

I recalled being party to a meeting of the high spirit council, which convened to decide what should be done. High spirit beings clothed in light gathered before a silver table surrounded by white, marble-like pillars. No shadows here, and no temperature. The colour of their garments denoted their standing in the community. As I remembered this, the vision pulled at my heart. If I could show you a glimpse through the keyhole of what this place is like you would strive so hard to get there and never want to leave. With this setting in mind and the understanding that whoever was appointed this task would no doubt be ridiculed, you will see why the prospect of this assignment was not a popular one.

Eventually the decision was made and I was allocated the job. Several others were chosen to help. In an age of advancing technology, reaching people should be easy. No standing on hilltops telling stories now, there would be theatres, newspapers, radio, internet and television. It seemed I was to be a twentieth-century prophet; the trouble is that where people would once listen to prophets because there was little else to do, now there would be information overload and my small voice could easily get lost. The challenge was to reach as many people as possible, so at least they would be given the opportunity to take the right path. I knew that even if they did not believe me or indeed if they mocked me, I must fall to my knees for all people.

On my last morning in the hills, I awoke surrounded by a kind of peace. Strength emanated from the very rocks as I breathed in the bracken and exhaled pure calm. The Creator was all around me, and I found quiet comfort in Him as I took rest before my journey home. I wondered how people could ever doubt His presence when His miracles surround us. The precise engineering of the human body, the cocktail of elements that allow life in all things, the rolling dance of the planets. How can they not see Him in all of this? The answer was as apparent as the carpet of purple heather which now lay before me. If you stand close up against the face of a mountain and describe what you can see, you would perhaps give an account of stone, abstract greyness, a barren expanse of rock. You could not from this vantage point see the mountain. It is too big and too close. So it is with God. Man often cannot see Him. He is too big and too close.

I understood things much better after this period of meditation, and now I knew what I must do, but the world around me seemed strange. I was not the same person I was before, although David Drew was still a part of me. I still remembered my childhood and this life, but now there were other clear memories too, shining through like facets of my soul. I got into the car and headed home.

Jane was happy I was home, although she eyed me suspiciously. She could see something was different. I wasn't distressed anymore, which was obviously a relief to her, but I could tell she had noticed a deeper change. It troubled me that my wife was hesitant and less familiar when we spoke. I gave her a kiss that said everything was alright, but things were a little peculiar.

I was aware that some of my mannerisms had changed and set to work correcting the issue. I told a corny joke or two to show that I was still the same, but the delivery was awkward somehow, and her alarmed expression showed me it needed work. I had to focus on the David part of me if I was to pull this off without freaking everyone out. I looked into the mirror and studied my face. I didn't think my appearance had changed, but Jane said that something behind my eyes was different. She took my face in her hands and asked where the man she married was. I smiled and reassured her that he was in here somewhere. Her silence told me she remained unconvinced.

"Don't think I'm someone else. It's still me. I wouldn't leave you."

It took a week or two, but I learned to behave like just David again. I got into the swing of things and life went on pretty much as normal, despite my being an odd hybrid of heaven and Earth. I still had physical needs, unlike my colleagues in the spirit world, and I learned to shelve the enormity of the accumulation when I thought my brain needed a break. Pepe gave me a suggestion on how to succeed. "Work, rest and play in equal balance". It sounded like a chocolate bar commercial, but it proved to be invaluable advice. It was odd at first, but eventually, I managed to perfect having one foot in each world.

As 1988 drew to a close, we decided to end the year with a short break in St. Andrews. It had been a wild and wonderful year. We had not visited Scotland for some time, the nearest being a venue I appeared at in the Lake District, where we found ourselves snowed into a cosy B&B with open fires and superb home cooking. It was the most agreeable disaster I ever encountered.

St. Andrew's is a historic university town on Scotland's east coast. It is famous for its golf, so we booked three days in the Rusacks Hotel on the Old Course. The drive took longer than we anticipated, largely down to the scarcity of Scottish motorways. It was dark by the time we arrived, and the girls were sleeping soundly in the back seat. The sea roared and broke hard against the rocks as our imposing destination loomed monochrome above us like Castle Dracula.

Inside was a different story. We carried the girls through the lobby to the glow and crackle of open fires. Ornate plaster décor and the largest gilded seascapes I had ever seen framed the spectacular centrepiece, an eight foot Christmas tree flanked by leather wingback chairs. This was a welcome haven from the long, bleak journey.

We spent our time in Scotland eating, soaking in the bath and walking St. Andrews' quaint square of shops and cafes. The weather was bitter and the coastline harsh, but that just made listening to the crackling fire while we sipped our brandies and hot chocolates seem all the more decadent.

On the second evening as we sat in the lounge my peace was interrupted. Jane was fiddling with the silverware, chatting about Christmas presents, when her words began to fall away. Her lips were still moving, and waiters bustled attentively around us, but the room was silent. I could see a huge aeroplane, not through the window but as though it was on a cinema screen. As I wondered why I was seeing this, there was a flash. The nose of the plane broke off, and the fuselage broke into pieces, falling and disintegrating in a ball of fire. Seconds later the scene was gone, and waiters were removing silver domes to reveal our dinner in one slick and synchronised movement. I had suddenly lost my appetite.

As I described to Jane what I had seen, her eyes widened and she suggested we should phone someone. I had no idea where or when or indeed if this would happen. Who could we phone and what could we say? I prayed this was a mistake, and we tried to put it out of our minds as best we could.

The following day was December 21st. As we were dressing for the evening, the TV in our room was tuned into the news. Jane saw it first, shouting for me to come out of the bathroom. Pan Am flight 103 from Frankfurt to Detroit had exploded in the air over Scotland. We watched in silence.

The next day on our journey home we had to pass the crash site at Lockerbie. Craters and debris on the dual carriageway had closed the southbound lanes. There was the sense of a town in mourning, the world in mourning. Fatalities included 189 Americans, 43 British, and 38 people from 18 other countries, a total of 270 dead. At the time it was the worst act of terror the United States had encountered, September 11th being yet to come. Students were travelling home for Christmas, 16 crew members and 11 residents of Lockerbie, who perished when the flaming debris landed on their homes. The terrorist bomb which caused the explosion was intended to detonate over the Atlantic, where evidence would be hard to retrieve, but the flight was late taking off. Had the plane been on time the town of Lockerbie would have been unscathed.

Some potential passengers had overslept, missed the flight or changed their reservations in a turn of fate that saved their lives. These reportedly included actress Kim Cattrall, singing group The Four Tops, tennis champion Mats Wilander and Johnny Rotten of the Sex Pistols.

Terrorist acts are the worst kind of atrocity. In wars, soldiers fight soldiers, and the awful tragedy of civilian casualties is either accidental or incidental. Terrorism deliberately targets the innocent, usually without demands or ransom. Often their acts are carried out in the name of

God. What a blasphemy! If these misguided people could only see the terrible place they will find themselves in when their time is up, they would surely change their ways.

Although we all follow different pathways, we can still learn from each other if we choose not to judge. There is a roundabout on the busy Wolverhampton Road in Birmingham where a Sikh guru used to live in a makeshift tent. He could be found here in summer and winter alike. People of all cultures would visit him, listen to his wisdom and bring him gifts.

The homeless man hears every sound, observes everything. In our busy lives, we rush around in our suits, too wrapped up in urgent triviality to notice the world around us. If we removed our footwear and felt the grass beneath our feet for just half an hour each day, we would benefit tremendously. Because people are not like us, it does not mean they have nothing to teach us.

Religions should be able to live side by side in harmony. If your faith makes you hostile toward others, it's time to look for a new path. When you find yourself thinking that others deserve to die simply because their beliefs differ from yours, alarm bells should ring. There are many roads to God. The importance is not in the detail but in how we love each other. This is how to love Him, and it is how you will be measured.

Spirit Planes

Dr Albert Schweitzer

Devastation at Lockerbie

With Ricky

Family life before the accumulation

Llandudno beach

Pilgrimage to Jerusalem

On TV & Radio in Denmark

The unpredicted arrival of baby John

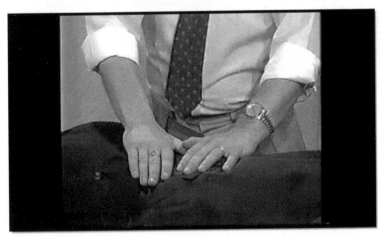

Healing on TV

With Ricky and Maureen

Blue Cloud Lodge, murder house turned Spiritual Centre

The Marlborough Arms, The most haunted pub in Chester.

Bart

Kilroy

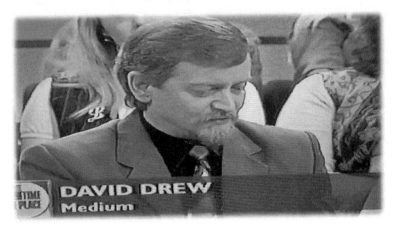

The Time, The Place

8

A Hand with the Healing

I have always been cautious when recommending other clairvoyants. There is a huge responsibility in putting someone's life and emotions under the influence of another. After a demonstration at Blackpool's North Pier, I was horrified when two seaside fortune tellers approached me to ask what I tell the 'punters'. Since then I have had little respect for tarot card and crystal ball readers. I don't understand why anyone would need props if they are actually psychic. I cannot abide con artists who discredit all the good work of genuine mediums. It is more than bank balances they damage. A dental receptionist once told me that when she had her tarot cards read, the fortune teller turned them over one by one, explaining what each card meant. When he came to the third card, he said, "While you are on holiday this summer your husband will die." He then carried on as if he had just told her she was going to misplace a favourite handbag. The poor woman was distraught and had an awful holiday waiting for her husband to drop dead, which of course he did not.

I am not a fortune teller. Having said that I do, with the help of those in spirit, give advice on the future. From where they are they can see more clearly the direction in which we are headed, the pathway we are on at the moment. I may be able to tell someone that the way things are going, they will be emigrating to Canada for example. Along with that information, I will give advice. Perhaps this is a good thing; maybe it would be a disaster and they need to change direction. If your future was pre-determined as fortune tellers would have you believe we would go through this life like robots. Decisions we make affect our future, and regardless of any influence from spirit, we should make up our own minds. Unless the answers come from those in high spirit, you should give the advice of those who have passed on the same consideration you would if they were still here.

Sitters often ask me what is going to happen. The simple truth is that if you continue to do what you have always done the results will continue to be the same. If you plant daffodil bulbs, do not be surprised when daffodils grow. We reap what we sow. If you want a change then plant something different, try something new.

Even genuine, well-meaning mediums are not infallible. Some are more highly developed than others; a few may become tempted to cheat in high-pressure situations, and all can make mistakes. When I hear spirit, for example, the words are not always clear. It can be like listening to a crackly old radio. In addition to this, signs and symbols can be misinterpreted. A road branching in two directions is the sign of a parting, but is this a death, a divorce or someone moving overseas? Sometimes the person I am hearing is not the same one I am seeing, and that can be confusing. Before giving a reading I point out to the sitter that I do make mistakes, but I always tell the truth of what I see. Above all, great care should always be taken when delivering sensitive information. Words affect lives.

When it came to choosing guest mediums for the psychic club I did so with as much caution as possible. It was not easy to fill all the dates as there were fewer genuine candidates than you might imagine. This shortage resulted in several being booked for more than one appearance. Occasionally, after being introduced to the psychic club, the mediums would come along and regularly sit in the audience, just to enjoy the atmosphere and be among like-minded people. On one such occasion when I was on stage, roles were reversed, and I found myself on the receiving end of a surprising message.

Many spirit doctors have worked with me over the years. One doctor tends to be more prominent, with others stepping in perhaps to apply their expertise regarding specific medical conditions. They stay with me for months or years and then move on.

One morning as I welcomed my first healing appointment of the day, I noticed a new doctor. He was an elderly gentleman with a bushy, grey moustache and he was very much taking the lead. He wore a white shirt and a spotted bow tie. Sections of his tousled hair, which was swept casually back, escaped in wild rebellion across his forehead. His manner was serious, but his eyes seemed kind. Throughout the healing session, he stood beside me, and I remember observing that we seemed a good fit, instantly working together well.

At the end of the day, before taking his leave of me, he introduced himself as Dr Albert. I thanked him for his help, and we said a short prayer together.

Albert was prominent in most of my healing sessions after that and was relentless in his determination to keep working. A week or so after he joined me, a lady came with stomach problems. She settled on the antique doctor's couch I had acquired some years earlier at auction, and I stood at her side, allowing my eyes to close. I extended my hands across her belly, took some deep breaths and relaxed to enable me to focus exclusively on spirit. I always play soft piano music to aid relaxation, and as the healing began Albert moved closer and closer until we were occupying the same space, his hands over mine. I opened my eyes a moment later to find I was sitting at my desk, and the lady was no longer on the bed, but wide-eyed in the chair opposite.

There was a pause before she asked if I was alright. I wasn't quite sure. I was disorientated and it took a few minutes for me to realise that I had been hijacked. It seemed Dr Albert liked to work quite literally 'hands-on'. Initially, I felt a little put out. Uninvited he had used my body to do the healing while I was in a trance state. What is more, the woman proceeded to ask me about things I had said. Mortified I realised that he had been speaking with her! Apparently, he told her, "We cannot put back what has been taken away". She asked if I was referring the section of bowel which had been removed. She had not previously shared this information with me, and I had no idea what to say. I changed the subject to hide my embarrassment, pretending nothing out of the ordinary had happened. She must have been terribly confused as I hurriedly showed her to the door, pointing out the nearest bus stop.

With time I grew accustomed to the way the new doctor preferred to work, and Albert, or Uncle Albert as the children came to call him after a having healing for tummy aches and the like, soon felt like one of the family. Mostly he liked to work while I was in deep trance, and in some cases would even perform psychic surgery, which was new territory for me. He came to exercise exceptional control. Patients reported hearing clicking sounds as instruments were passed hand to hand. I would close my eyes momentarily, see a light, then it would be gone and so was I. Parts of me would begin to feel numb, like I was surrendering to anaesthetic, before I drifted off into what seemed like a deep sleep. For some patients I would work in semi-trance. Dr Albert would step in and move my hands while I relaxed but remained conscious. On the occasions when he didn't occupy my body, patients would often report feeling a second pair of hands on them while mine were resting on their head. Results were good no matter how he chose to work and I decided it was not in anyone's interest for me to question his technique.

A few weeks later at Royalles, a lady medium was in the audience. When I had finished the talk, she approached me, bearing a pint and a very strange message.

"I have been looking at a man standing next to you. I am sure it's Albert Schweitzer!"

I tried not to look obtuse. Although the name was familiar, I had no idea who Albert Schweitzer was. I took a sip of my beer and cautiously confirmed I had a doctor in spirit called Dr Albert who helped with the healing. She described him with some excitement. It sounded like Albert alright, could this be true? I mentioned it to Jane, who had heard the name but had only a vague idea of who he was and no clue what he looked like. I wanted to ask him if this was true, but my enthusiastic new doctor was suddenly conspicuous by his absence.

I casually asked around to see if people had heard of Albert Schweitzer, without revealing the reason for my interest. An old man in the local pub mentioned that Madame Tussaud's Waxworks on the promenade housed a likeness of him in the medical section. That weekend I took the family. We skipped over Michael Jackson and Jack Duckworth, and at last there he was. Albert was looking back at me from a display about the hospital he built in French Equatorial Africa. The plaque said he died in 1969.

"It was 1965," he corrected over my shoulder. "But I'm more alive now than I have ever been."

"Why on earth didn't you tell me who you are?" I was turning over in my mind how many more people might come for help if they knew who the doctor was.

"It is not the worker that is important but the work the worker does."

Of course, he was right. There are no famous people in spirit. Notoriety holds no significance there.

As he seemed unwilling to discuss himself, I decided to do a little reading. Albert was born in 1875 in Kayserberg, Alsace-Lorraine, which belonged to Germany at the time but subsequently became French. He was the son of a parson and at the age of eighteen went to Strasbourg University. In 1900 on the completion of his licentiate in theology, he was ordained as curate. He also studied music and by the age of twenty-eight he was the principal of the college. As a proficient organist, he was called upon to take the place of the church organist at Gunsbach at the young age of nine. He wrote many books on music, theology and philosophy. I mentioned to him one day that I was thinking of reading a book he wrote entitled, 'The Quest of the Historical Jesus'. *"Leave it alone,"* was his response. *"I understand things better now than I ever did then.*

Miracles happen all around us, but they go unseen. We look upon the same stars that people have looked upon for thousands of years. God's creation is perfect. Man made things come and go – not God's. God waters the flowers and looks after all things – even us. People care more for the flowers in the garden than the people in the fields. Colour is not important. We are all God's creations."

In 1911 at the age of thirty-six, he qualified as a doctor of medicine and went to work in a Parisian hospital. In 1913 he left Western civilisation for Lambarene in French

Equatorial Africa, where he built and sustained a mission hospital. He took with him seventy cases of medical supplies and a piano. Here his studies and work on leprosy made him world famous.

In 1952 he received the Nobel Peace Prize for his philosophy, 'Reverence for Life'. He died in 1965 and was buried at his Lambarene hospital, in a grave marked by the cross he himself made.

After his passing Dr Albert began to work in spirit hospitals, tending to those who had died in an earthly hospital after a long illness and found themselves in similar surroundings upon passing. Often they did not comprehend that they no longer had a physical disease, or indeed a physical body. His desire to heal led him to look for a medium through which he could continue to work, alongside other spirit helpers, such as my good friend Yeung. He once told me, "When the right hand tires, use the left, but never tire of using the brain." In life and the afterlife, it seems Dr Schweitzer is ever the workaholic. Months passed and in due course a longstanding spiritualist newspaper 'The Psychic News' expressed an interest in interviewing me. I was initially reluctant to mention Albert. Working with this notorious doctor still seemed rather unbelievable even to me, although he would modestly insist that the honour was his. On the other hand, if the publicity helped us to reach more people, surely it could only be a good thing? It was a dilemma. I bit the bullet, braced myself for ridicule and told the reporter about my latest spirit doctor. The journalist was fascinated, and on hearing about him arranged for a friend to join us when we met. This lady had been told she was going blind but didn't believe in spiritual healing. She agreed to come with her colleague and try it out, but only because she was intrigued, having admired Dr Schweitzer since girlhood.

The finished article testified how Albert told her he had drained her eye and also confirmed that this was the exact course of treatment her doctors had recommended. She was also amazed that he wished her many happy returns for the birthday they shared on the 14th January. The report went on to say that her eyesight had already improved. I was relieved to hear that despite her scepticism, her experience had been a positive one.

Before she left, the journalist had taken telephone numbers of some willing patients who were happy to share their experiences. One lady told the paper how her mother in intensive care was not expected to live past the weekend, but five days after we gave her healing she was sitting up in bed knitting, and went on to make a full recovery. Another, who suffered from severe, long-term depression after a horrific start in life, spoke of feeling vibration and an intense heat coming from my hands. She went on to say, "I feel on top of the world now and want to thank God for giving me this experience because now I can help so many people around me who are depressed or unhappy."

When the article hit the newsstands, requests for healing converged upon me with startling intensity. In the midst of the mayhem, I was surprised to receive a letter from a lady who introduced herself as the widow of John Leslie, a healer who had previously been operating out of Brighton on the south coast.

Dear Mr Drew,

A friend of mine brought my attention to the article about you in Psychic News, which I read with great interest. My own dear husband, John, was also used by Dr Albert Schweitzer for a long time before he died on the 15th August 1987. When I read the description of how he works with you, I became very excited, for I could have been reading of his work with John. Every detail you give is the same. What a wonderful thing that his work is continuing. I feel so happy and thankful that this is happening. If you will consider a moment, you will realise that not only have I lost John's physical presence (not of course his real self, which I am always aware of), but I miss very much the band of workers who taught and healed through him, and who had become familiar and dear to me. We also had a circle for many years. There were eight of us, harmonious and loving. I still keep in touch with them all, of course, but I do miss our circle.

The doctor liked to work in trance when necessary, as he does with you. I have 'sat in' many times with people who were perhaps a little nervous, and many times I have been aware of the instruments and the assistants. My friend Mary, of our circle, was also aware of the ticking of the doctor's old fashioned pocket watch. I wonder if anyone with you will hear it. As with you, we were told several times by different mediums that they could see Dr Schweitzer with John – usually they had no idea that he was working with him, so we had ample confirmation of his presence.

John had a most interesting experience. He was invited to Alsace to give healing to people in the region, and while there he was taken by car to the doctor's old home in Kayserberg. I have a beautiful little bust of the doctor which came from his home. We thought how amazing that this had happened, of all the places in the world it just came about that he was taken there.

I hope you will not mind me writing to you. I felt very much the impulse to do so, and feel that John would very much have liked to meet you. He is probably with you sometimes anyway, as I am sure he is now working with his spirit friends.

With every good wish for the future,

Sincerely yours,

Joyce Leslie

Apparently, I was not Dr Albert's first port of call. The dates Joyce gave me suggested he had sought me out when John passed away, leaving him in need of a new channel to work through. It was a fascinating letter, and I instantly developed an affection for this lovely lady.

A few months later I was booked to work in Portsmouth. As I would be travelling to the south coast, I took the opportunity to arrange a meeting with Mrs Leslie. Maureen, who drove me there at her usual breakneck speed, accompanied me to the airy foyer of the Grand Hotel on Brighton seafront. We ordered a pot of tea for three, taking in the ornate décor as we waited for Joyce to join us. She arrived right on time, her eyes immediately twinkling when she saw us. It was evident how much she missed Dr Albert and how happy she was to have some link with him again. The slightly built lady cast off her long, grey coat and settled down beside us like an old friend. We chatted for an hour or so about her late husband's work as well as the character and quirks of the good doctor. Then she invited us to visit her home to see the room where they used to work. It was just a short drive away and we accepted the invitation gratefully.

The house was charming, with a suggestion of lavender in the air and a wonderfully tranquil atmosphere. When we entered John's healing room, she made straight for a shelf. And took down an object. She cradled it for a moment then handed it to me. It was the small carved bust of Albert which had been presented to her husband by the Albert Schweitzer Trust when he visited Alsace. She explained that she wanted it to stay with Dr Albert and thought I should take it. I was incredibly moved by the gesture. The statue remains to this day in pride of place by the healing bed where Albert works.

As demand for the healing grew, I opened new clinics around the country in addition to the ones I held in Blackpool and Preston. One weekend I would be in Edinburgh, at the Royal Hospital for Sick Children, the next in an alternative therapy clinic in London's Primrose Hill. I was even called upon to give healing to a foal with bad knees!

I could only see ten to twelve people at each session before I was completely exhausted. Each patient would drain me until I was like an old battery with nothing left to give. Albert, on the other hand, would have gladly had me work all day. He was even more tireless now than he was in life. The success of the clinics reached the ears of researchers at Capital Radio and BBC Radio Scotland, who invited me to hold a regular phone in show. Time with Jane and the girls had to be squeezed in between travelling, local appointments and the Psychic Club, but it felt good to be reaching more people. I enjoyed a tangible sense of achievement that I was doing what I was supposed to do in spreading the word to a wider audience. Radio reporters visited a few of my patients and recorded interviews with them. Jane taped them for me to hear later.

Mrs G; *"My daughter went and had healing. She had a snapped cartilage in her knee. She went to the doctor, and he said she would have to have an operation. She got into the hospital to have the operation and when she was there she saw another lady that had already had it in terrible distress, and she didn't want to go through all that. After about two weeks it was still very painful. I said she should go and see David for healing, which she did. It hurt for two days afterwards and after that, she had no trouble at all."*

Andrea; *"When I first went to David Drew about a year ago, I originally went because of the psychic meetings, I didn't know about healing or anything like that. When I went I got told by him that I'd got problems in my lower* stomach. I had already seen a doctor. I'd had an operation the year before on my womb and had told the doctor I didn't want to go for another operation. I went to David for the healing. At first, I felt stupid but after the first couple of times, I started to feel better. I went back to my own doctor. They could find nothing at all wrong with me."

Catherine; "I first went to see David Drew about six months ago. My sister recommended him to me as my baby has cystic fibrosis. I didn't really believe in it at first, but every time my baby went she started putting on weight, I kept her free of chest infections, everything just pointed to it working. The doctor at the hospital said there is no hope for her; she could die by the time she is twenty-five. I can't stand by and watch my baby die. I have got to try something. David is convinced he can cure her. He told me that every evening at ten o'clock that Dr Albert would come to her and heal her absently. I get her up about 9.45 each night and no matter what she is doing, at ten o'clock on the dot she just stares into space, as though there is somebody there."

Eileen; "I went with the view, if I come out no different I have lost nothing, so why not? So I went in and explained everything to David that had happened and he said to make myself comfortable in a chair. He put on some music then he came over and laid his hands on my shoulder. At this *point, his voice altered. His Welsh accent completely disappeared, and it was a very gentlemanly voice, very professional. He laid his hand on my shoulder and down my arm, and it was like a nice, warm, soothing sensation down my arm. He did the same with my hand. A few minutes after that he just told me to sit there and be still for a minute. I must admit I did feel very, very emotional. When he'd finished he told me to raise my left arm, and my arm went straight up, which I couldn't believe! Then he told me to make a fist. When I went in I couldn't make a fist, or even quarter of a fist but my fingers went straight down to the palm of my hand. I just couldn't believe it!"*

Things quickly gathered pace, and next I found myself invited to appear on TV chat shows such as 'The Time, The Place', 'Kilroy' and 'Esther', who were good enough to invite me back several times. All promised to be excellent vehicles to help spread the word, despite the heated debate. Not everyone accepted the work I did but I was more than prepared to fight my corner.

'Kilroy' was a BBC One daytime chat show hosted by politician turned presenter, Robert Kilroy-Silk. It was broadcast live, and ran for one hour, covering topical or controversial subjects. The shows I appeared on consisted of discussions on spiritual healing; the first being entitled, 'A Healer Changed My Life'. Maureen came to that one with me and spoke about the positive outcome of her healing. Others who had been similarly helped were in the audience and told their stories. To balance the debate, there was a politician and a doctor who claimed that all these people had experienced spontaneous remission. From my view, people came to see me and went away well. If they wanted to call it coincidence, that might be far-fetched but it was not the end of the world. They could call it what they like as long as the patient was better. I never suggested that anyone should visit a healer instead of a doctor and I could not understand the vehement opposition. My argument was, there is no reason why we cannot all work together to make people well.

Kilroy, who usually came across as a pleasant and reasonable man, surprised me at one point by asking a healer in the audience why he charged for his services if he had a genuine gift, then asked another, who had a day job, why he worked if he truly had a gift. Surely Kilroy could see that we have the need to eat and pay bills just like doctors, vicars and everyone else.

'Esther' was a show on BBC Two, hosted by Esther Rantzen, a journalist and TV presenter. This was also filmed live, but the format was a little different. I was part of a panel on stage who engaged in debate with members of the audience. The show carried the title, 'Contacting the

Dead', and I shared the stage with Dr Helen Haste, Professor of Psychology, Dr Raj Persaud, Consultant Psychiatrist and a lady who had recorded some spirit voices on tape.

The next television invitation came from 'The Time, The Place', a half-hour chat show on ITV, hosted by presenter John Stapleton. I travelled to Glasgow or London to appear on shows which discussed such topics as healing or hauntings. Audience members told stories of how Ouija Boards had attracted 'ghosts 'into their homes. One man, in a dark coat and hat was presumed by one woman to be an intruder, until he vanished before her eyes. Another lady was violently dragged out of bed towards the window. She later discovered the previous tenant had fallen to her death from that window in unexplained circumstances.

An HTV show called, 'Weird Wales', heard how people were travelling to Llandudno to receive healing from a dead doctor, and came to Blue Cloud Lodge to film him at work. I welcomed each and every way to promote our message, but the next invitation caused me to hesitate.

James Whale is a television and radio presenter whose success was founded on his frank and opinionated style. Some would call it plain speaking, others bad manners but either way it got people's attention. His late night TV show was controversial to say the least, and when I was asked to appear, I knew this was going to be a particularly rough ride. The subject of the show was to be alternative medicine, and James would interview me on the topic of spiritual healing. I had to decide if I was prepared to face the inevitable ridicule. It could backfire in a huge way. When James Whale heard about Albert Schweitzer he would have a field day! No-one ever said this would be an easy task, and I could not with clear conscience reject off hand the opportunity to reach such a broad audience. I took a breath and accepted the invitation to appear.

It was live TV, and Jane watched nervously from home, pacing the floor as the titles rolled. The opening shot was James Whale introducing the show from a horizontal position as I placed my hands on his back. I like to think I managed to hold my own in the hard-hitting interviews that followed. James Whale did have a good-natured dig at Dr Albert and the fact that I charged an extortionate £10 for a consultation, but people called the show to say that after watching me on the programme their backaches and headaches had disappeared. The producers were impressed and invited me back to appear on another show, this time, to talk about life after death.

I felt a sense of achievement that I was reaching people on a grander scale, but I knew more was expected of me. It was not nearly enough. If I appeared on stage seven days a week, there would still be scope to do more. However, if I wrote a book, not only would it attract a whole new and much wider audience, but the message I came to deliver could still be circulating the globe long after I leave it. This was quite clearly the next step.

I knocked together a synopsis and approached a literary agent, who sent it out to several publishers. Eventually, we found one who was happy to commission the book and pay a small advance so that I could take time out to make some progress with the content. This was going to be a time-consuming project and, although I was sure of everything I wanted to say, I was not confident of being able to continue with my heavy workload and still complete the book within the publisher's six-month deadline.

My agent had a solution. He recommended a young journalist who could act as a ghost writer (no pun intended). I yielded to his experience and took the advice. I invested a good deal of my time over the next few months with the allocated writer as she made notes about my life and the message I was hoping to convey. Then, at last, she went away to write, promising to deliver the book to me chapter by chapter so that I could make any alterations.

Months passed and despite her promises, no manuscript arrived. She became increasingly difficult to reach and as the deadline drew near I realised with some trepidation that a huge obstacle could well have been placed in my path. The girl assured me that the book would be ready, and I stressed that I needed time to assess her work and make any changes. It was so important that the message was accurate, and I could not be sure that she had completely understood my words without seeing her work. I realised with a knot in my stomach that I had been naïve to lay such an important project in the hands of a stranger.

At last, with just one week to go a hard copy of the completed manuscript arrived in the post. I made a cup of tea, lit a cigarette and carefully opened the long-awaited envelope. As I turned the pages, my heart broke. It was horribly inaccurate. The girl had written that I felt a scream rise in my throat during trance when of course I am not capable of feeling anything in this state, and page after page of sensationalised drivel lay before me like carnage on a battlefield. In the race to produce a book, truth had fallen at the first hurdle.

The publisher was more than happy with the finished article. It was an interesting read, and he was sure it would sell, but how could I allow it to go to press? I paid the journalist off and went back to square one. No one understood that this was not a mere money-making exercise, it was about reaching as many people as possible with potential life changing information.

I began again, disappointed at my failure but undefeated. I was determined to put the message into print. I had to succeed in this. In just a few weeks I produced a kind of reference book for anyone who was interested in learning about the meaning of life and what happens after death. I deliberately made it easy to read so that nothing would be too complicated for anyone of any intellectual level to understand and I laid the content out so that the reader could open it at any chapter and not be confused. Entitled 'Stairway to Heaven' the book covered questions people frequently asked me about reincarnation, poltergeists, the spirit world and I added a kind of map showing how to live life so as to avoid the pits.

The release of Stairway generated massive attention, for a variety of reasons. Regional branches of W H Smith invited me to hold book signing events in their stores. The launch was organised at the Blackpool branch. Queues of people came to have their copy signed, and reporters were there to cover the event. Seeing the message in print, at last, was a fantastic feeling. I was well received at all the signings until it came to W H Smith in Preston. The previous event had been their Wrexham, North Wales store. It had been a successful venture, and in the hour I was there we sold over fifty copies. However, before I arrived, a minister entered the store and made a complaint. He told him that my book was controversial and attacked religion, although I doubt very much that he had read it. When the manager of the Preston branch heard of this confrontation, he immediately began to panic, cancelling the signing session and refusing to stock the book. Once again the church was obstructing me.

I admit I was taken off guard by the amount of negative attention Stairway to Heaven seemed to attract. In the furore that followed, I was invited to join the Anglican and Catholic Bishops of Liverpool on Radio Merseyside one Sunday afternoon for a contentious debate. By now I was accustomed to radio and welcomed the opportunity to get my point across.

As I pulled into the studio car park, a dishevelled gentleman who turned out to be the presenter was pacing up and down on the steps looking anxious. It seems that when the bishops realised that I would be on the show, they refused at the last minute to participate. It was due to air in fifteen minutes, and the studio was in a flap.

"It's ok," I patted the presenter on the shoulder, "We can just do an interview or a phone in instead if you like." He let out a relieved sigh.

"I was hoping you might be prepared to go ahead on your own. Thank you so much."

We began the show with a chat about how I first discovered I was psychic, and then the calls came in.

The first caller was a lady named Doreen. When her mother passed away twelve months previously, she bought two bunches of fragrant mixed freesia. She placed one in the coffin and the other in the home in readiness for the funeral. On several occasions afterwards, when Doreen was feeling low, she suddenly smelled freesia, often in her home, but sometimes in random locations such as when she was out shopping. The fragrance left her feeling comforted and uplifted. Doreen had never told anyone about this and wanted to ask me if this really was down to her mother.

I explained that when someone in spirit is unable to make their presence known in any other way, then bringing a familiar smell, such as perfume or pipe tobacco is common, as it is an easier way to communicate than learning to show themselves. They may also be able to move things, such as photographs, in an attempt to get your attention. I told her she should talk to her mum when this happens as I was certain she was there with her.

The DJ asked why people are so reluctant to share their psychic experiences with others, and it raised and interesting point. Far more people experience premonitions, hauntings and strange foreboding feelings than you might think. They tend not to talk about them for fear of ridicule, they come to me with their stories because they know I will understand. If all these people spoke openly, they would realise that these are common phenomena and perhaps the subject would be viewed with more credibility.

9
Coming Home

My years in Blackpool were fuelled with hope and inspiration. Foundations were strong beneath my feet, and I began to believe I might be equipped to achieve what was expected of me. When the lease on our home came to an end, rather than look for another house in the North West of England, I yearned to take the family home to Wales. My sister Annette now lived in the area, and we holidayed there often. The children always bounced around with excitement at the mention of our Welsh jaunts, and Jane had fallen completely in love with Llandudno, a small seaside town just down the road from where I used to live. The town was named for the church of its patron Saint Tudno. Cormorants roosted on Llandudno's limestone cliffs and peregrine falcons, rare as the wild cotoneaster that grew there, nested in their secluded habitat high above the town. Settlements in the area dated back to the Stone Age, and tunnels of a Bronze Age copper mine excavated by 4,000-year-old hands, still meandered through the rock like old men's veins. The large seaside community made its home on the once submerged flatlands that stretch from mainland to mountain. It was the perfect area to live, with countryside, beaches and a network of shopping streets - a rarity in most isolated Welsh beauty spots. It was easy to see why Llandudno was known as the 'Queen of the Welsh Resorts'. This would be an idyllic place for the girls to grow up.

We found a timeworn three story house to rent while we looked for a property to buy. Our new home was at the foot of the Great Orme, the mountain which sits like a fingernail on the end of the peninsula. The Tudor style Maes Gwyn was in the style of a black and white half-timbered house and was close to an old stone built school which was perfect for the children. As a herald of inclement weather, the majestic Kashmiri goats which roam the wilds of the Orme would migrate to the lower, more sheltered slopes and were often to be found on misty winter mornings chewing privet in our front garden. Dead eyes under devil's horns surveyed us as we passed to take the girls to school, but they remained nonchalant, unruffled by our presence.

The pathway through the square garden led up to an imposing, black front door with a large central knob. Once inside the staircase swept down onto a vintage parquet floor. There was already a harmonious spirit presence there when we moved in. A young lady, pretty in full-length Victorian dress, often smiled up at me from the foot of the stairs, and there was other paranormal activity. My shaving mirror would occasionally jump across the room when Jane was making tea in the kitchen until finally in one last over-enthusiastic effort it smashed on the tiled floor. In the bathroom the light pull cord would often be extended horizontally across the high, corniced ceiling, looping itself down through the centre of the light shade. I had to fetch a stepladder each time to retrieve it. Also if one of us was alone watching TV, it was not uncommon for channels to change when we left the room to answer the doorbell, which had seemingly pressed itself.

Grey squirrels played in the high-walled back garden, where a small forgotten gravestone lay supine on the grass. An ordinary family might have been put off by these odd quirks and disturbances, but we loved that house. I made no attempt to evict our spirit friends as I had no sense that anyone was unhappy, and we were certainly content to share our living space. In any case, you could argue it was more their house than ours. Had it been for sale we would have bought it in a heartbeat.

The large empty bedroom on the third floor was ideal for holding circles. Often we used it as a place to simply be alone and pray. Because it was so peaceful we christened it 'the chapel'. The tranquil atmosphere in the room wrapped around everyone who entered like a warm blanket. When you stepped inside, the presence of high spirit was unmistakable.

Incidents of paranormal channel hopping began to increase, and I noticed that the TV seemed to flick back to the news channel repeatedly. The world news is filled today, just as it was then, with heart-wrenching stories that only reinforce the belief that humanity needs to change. The planet is being destroyed; religion is the excuse for all manner of atrocities and technology is advancing at the same alarming rate that spirituality is declining. At this time, the dominating story was the Gulf crisis.

President Saddam Hussain had been holding hundreds of British hostages in Baghdad as a human shield since Iraq invaded Kuwait in August 1990. I watched the plaintive images, women in tears, a child carrying a placard with the haunting caption, 'Let My Daddy Come Home'. I glanced at my girls playing with their Barbie dolls on the rug. Someone needed to do something for these people before war broke out. I thought about this for a few days, watching developments on TV and wondering what could be done. I felt an overwhelming urge to act, but why would anyone listen to me? Each time these negative thoughts entered my head, the answer I tried to dismiss was there in the shadows. It is the belief that we cannot change things that allows terrible situations to flourish. Ordinary people need to become involved, not just world leaders. If we all say, "What can I do? What is the point of trying?" nothing will ever be done. I could not in good conscience sit around while war loomed ever closer. I had to try something.

My first reaction was to approach the Gulf Support Group and offer myself as a hostage in place of a British man who was critically ill with cancer. This idea was dismissed as impractical, so I decided to try a spiritual solution. An attempt to avoid war and get the hostages released. Saddam Hussein did not fear President Bush or Mrs Thatcher, but he believed in one God and might just fear Him enough to back down over Kuwait. Regardless of how we worship in our respective countries, we surely had a starting point in this common belief. There is no such thing as a holy war, and God was no more on their side than that of the allied forces. He hates war and does not take sides in armed conflict. The whole of mankind are God's children and He only wants them to live together in peace.

I was shocked to hear that the Archbishop of Canterbury, Dr Robert Runcie, was quoted as saying that this war would be justifiable. If anyone talks in the name of God they should talk peace, not war. Instead of looking to military intervention, they must seek spiritual solutions, which can never come about while evil is fought with evil.

I wrote a carefully worded letter to Dr Azmi Shafiq Salihi, Ambassador at the Iraqi Embassy in London. I stated my intent to try to avert war and requested a meeting with his president. Jane thought I was out of my mind to think he would reply. When a letter inviting me to meet with the Ambassador arrived a week later, she was visibly concerned and fell suddenly silent. I packed a bag - and threw in my passport just in case.

There was a heavily armed military presence outside the Embassy when I arrived. As I climbed the steps I was aware my arrival had invoked a high level of curiosity from some unseen audience.   I detected the whisper of camera shutters, but no one attempted to stop me.

Standing exposed and conspicuous on the top step, I rang the bell and in due course was granted entry by a serious but courteous receptionist. The entrance hall was lofty and ornate, but I had little time to take it in before Dr Azmi Shafiq Salihi emerged from a reception room to greet me with arm outstretched. The tubby, balding gentleman approached me sporting a broad smile. I am not sure what I expected, but I was surprised by the Ambassador's friendly demeanour. After ordering coffee from the gentleman who had admitted me, he showed me into his office, where I sank with each step into the plush red carpet on route to the green leather Chesterfield, where I took a seat and tried to appear relaxed. The room was palatial and extravagant, more like a lounge than an office. We began with some small talk, how was my journey, that kind of thing. As he nodded and smiled through dark-rimmed spectacles, my attention faltered in favour of the huge gilt-framed photograph of Saddam above his desk. It was time to get to the point.

I began by explaining what I did, and my motives for wanting to travel to Baghdad. I primarily hoped to plead with President Hussein for the safe release of hostages, and to suggest that if he did not listen to me, he would lose his life. I spoke of how we are all members of the family of God, and how family members love each other despite their differences and do not point guns at each other but rather talk things through. I warned against the pointless carnage that war would bring, at the end of which would come a political compromise which could have been reached without loss of life. Mothers would lose sons, wives would lose husbands, and who could answer them when they asked what it was for?

The Ambassador was very accommodating and attentively listened until my soliloquy was finished, then he addressed me with a slow nod. He said he believed that I was indeed a man of God and added that he welcomed anything which might prevent war. He promised to pass on the letter I had written to his president and said he would be in touch soon regarding my travelling to Iraq to meet with him.

The letter was open so that he could examine its contents;

Dear Sir,

I write to you in the hope that you will believe what I have to say and act upon my words.

I understand that your people are very spiritual and respect God, the Almighty Creator of all things.

I was born for one purpose, to carry God's message of love and peace and to explain His natural laws. I know that you will agree that God is all knowing and all powerful. Today as most of the world stands united against you, I want to emphasise that even though you do not fear other world leaders, you must fear God.

The only solution to this crisis is a spiritual one. Military action will have drastic consequences, and this must be avoided. You, Mr President, hold within your hands the key to avoiding catastrophe, not only in the Middle East but worldwide. You can deliver peace and stability now, and in the future play your part in uniting nations in harmony. If you do not take notice of my words, thousands of lives will be needlessly lost, including your own, and the repercussions will be devastating.

You have a clear choice between bringing about peace and stability or war and division. I would welcome the opportunity of talking to you personally, and I would be willing to fly to Baghdad at a moment's notice if you would be prepared to listen to me. To bring about war and all that it entails will be easy, and that could be very soon. To bring about peace will be more difficult and will take longer.

Almighty God is watching you closely. He wants you to work towards finding a peaceful solution. He will walk at your side as you withdraw your troops and allow your foreign guests to return home. The world will then see that you do indeed seek peace, and any other grievances you have can be solved diplomatically. You would play your part on the world stage to bring unity to your region and would be doing God's will.

May God bless and guide you,

On the journey back to Wales I was fearful, but I had done what I needed to do, and hoped I would be under God's protection. I was aware that if I went to Baghdad and failed it would most likely result in my death. I waited for the call with bag packed, but within a matter of days it was clear it was too late. I was happy to hear that the hostages had been released at last, but a week or two later the coalition forces began dropping bombs to expel Iraqi military from Kuwait, and all hope for peace was lost. I knew that many parents would lose a child in this war, and families would question if it was worth it. There would be problems in the Middle East for years to come.

Jane and I were in no hurry to leave our haunted mansion, but we did expect to find a place to buy before the twelve-month lease expired. We procrastinated, taking time out to make a long awaited pilgrimage to Jerusalem before looking in earnest for our next home. By spring of 1992, we had still not agreed on a suitable place. I had a vague idea of finding somewhere that we could use as a spiritual centre. For some years I had been holding Psychic Weekends at various hotels across the country, during which there would be an evening of clairvoyance where I would pass on messages to the group from their loved ones in spirit, healing or psychic surgery sessions, an informative talk and on the last evening a séance. Llandudno would be the perfect place to hold these weekends without my having to travel. The town has a kind of primaeval energy oozing from its very rocks, making it conducive to spiritual reflection and contemplation. People could come to us from all over the world if we could just find a suitable property that fell within our budget.

It was a fresh spring morning, and the sun streamed in as I sat at the dining table in my jeans and sweater. I was slowly working my way through the Weekly News and a cooked breakfast when an advertisement on the property page caught my eye.

"The murder house goes up for auction today." I mused. "I might go along just to see how much it sells for."

Jane didn't see the point, but I had a rare day off so having nothing better to do I decided to go along. The auction was to be held at midday in Tudno castle, a large hotel in the town centre. When I arrived the room was already filling up and I took a seat on the front row.

The arrival of 1992 had been shrouded in sadness for the town. New Year celebrations were marred by the senseless murders of four people. Several others had been hospitalised in the horrific incident when a local taxi driver burst into his estranged wife's New Year party with a crowbar and a large knife. Her father was severely injured as he tried to prevent his son-in-law from entering the property, which had been a small hotel. The woman's sister was slashed with the knife as she tried to pass children to safety through an open window. Sadly his wife, who he had stabbed repeatedly, did not survive her injuries. Blood spattered children hysterically ran for help, which was slow to come amidst the mayhem of the town's New Year celebrations. The phone lines had been cut by the attacker as he passed through the house. Disturbed and desperate he then jumped into his car and took his own life in the most terrible way. He drove out of the town and swerved headlong into the path of an oncoming car. The vehicle was occupied by three teenagers on their way to a party. All four people were killed outright. It was a tragedy that left three children orphaned and struck Llandudno in the heart.

Since that terrible night, the hotel had been boarded up. It looked every bit the house of horror. People crossed the road rather than pass by it. The building was in danger of becoming a broken down monument to the brutal murders - a dark mark in the midst of an otherwise vibrant town.

I had never been to a property auction and was intrigued by the proceedings. Three properties were to be auctioned off before Clovelly House took its turn. The sad pariah was left until last. People raised their papers and scratched their noses as house after house found a new owner and there was only one left.

"I will open the bidding at £110,000. Who will start me off?"

The auctioneer's announcement was met with an embarrassing silence. He coaxed and cajoled, but no one flinched. He whispered to a man on his left and reduced the starting bid to £80,000. Still nothing. My hand was starting to twitch.

"Who will start me off with a bid?"

"£68,000!" The words were out of my mouth before I realised. A hum swept around the room, and I waited for the next bid. It didn't come. Oh, crap! Why did I do that? What would Jane say? What would my bank manager say? I waited for another bidder to break the silence but nothing came.

"Sold for £68,000!"

The deed was done. A hundred thoughts were spinning around in my head, but I tried to appear calm as I stood, hands shaking, to deliver a cheque for the required ten percent deposit. Cameras flashed. The press had come along to see if Clovelly House sold. They were apparently interested in whoever bought the 'house of horror', but when it sold to someone who talks to the dead, they saw the irresistible chance to sensationalise a simple story. I tried to explain to them that I had bought the hotel not *because* of what happened but in spite of it and that I hoped we would make it a happy house again.

When I arrived home, Jane was busy in the kitchen. "Did it sell?" she called out.

"Yes, yes. It sold" I tried to sound casual

"Who bought it?" Her voice was accompanied by the clatter of pots and the low rumble of a boiling kettle.

"We did!" I held my breath.

Her head appeared around the door, eyebrows raised.

I jingled the keys and smiled in an attempt to save myself. "Shall we take a look?"

Our new home was only a short walk away in the next street. Opposite the front gate, the station where passengers boarded the Victorian Great Orme Tramway hibernated until the spring when it would stir back to life. I fumbled for the key. The glass front door should have revealed the hallway inside, but all that remained of it were some glass shards which crunched beneath our feet. A large board was now nailed its place.

Inside it was dark and cold. The windows were covered, and the electricity had been disconnected. The carpets needed replacing, and the whole interior would certainly benefit from a facelift, but on the positive side, there were ten letting bedrooms, a lounge, a large bar and dining room. The potential was there for holding meetings and psychic weekends. There was even a room which would make an ideal office and healing room. It was perfect, well – at least we could make it perfect.

Jane rolled her eyes at my optimism. She was trying to rub fingerprint powder from a door frame with a crumpled tissue whilst eyeing the blood spattered stairwell with an air of resignation.

"A lick of paint and it will be fine! We could be open by Easter." I was deliberately upbeat but with Easter only six weeks away I doubt I was easing her concerns. This would certainly be a massive undertaking.

"You do remember I hate to cook?" I could tell she was trying to remain calm.

"You are an excellent cook! You can do anything. We can make this work!" I smiled, amused that the cooking phased her but the mass murder didn't.

Her eyes were searching my face for a glimmer of recognition that I was missing the point. I didn't bite. She looked around with a sigh then turned to go. "Get some paint. I'll make a start tomorrow."

We agreed to make as many changes as possible, so as to lay rest to the stigma. We re-named the hotel 'Blue Cloud Lodge' and with the help of an army of friends had the place spick and span by Easter. As I stood on reception welcoming the first guest on Good Friday, Jane was wiping away a last remaining splash of dried blood we had overlooked on the bottom glass panel of the dining room door. The hotel was up and running. Now we were ready for the next step. I needed to lay the foundation for a spiritual centre.

Blue Cloud Lodge became home to 'The British Academy of Spiritual Enlightenment', or 'B.A.S.E.'. My new venture encompassed psychic development classes, lectures, Psychic Weekends, a healing clinic, private readings and on the first Thursday of every month an evening of clairvoyance in the spacious lower ground floor bar.

I never saw the spirit of the lady of the house, which was a good sign. She had no doubt moved on to a new life in a new world. All was as it should be. The only signs of unusual activity were sporadic ghostly footsteps and certain doors which would mysteriously lock and unlock themselves. On one occasion a little wet blood was found on the kitchen door, even though no one had cut themselves, but these events soon petered out and gave way to nicer vibes from our high spirit friends. Before long the only spirits left within those walls were the ones that came with us. Blue Cloud Lodge was to be our family home for many years, and the one most fondly remembered by our children.

When Ayesha reached fourteen, she was old enough to sit in my weekly development circle. Within a few months, she was beginning to see some things from time to time. Her artistic flair meant that eventually, she was able to draw the guides and helpers of some of the sitters.

Sian was too young to sit in circle, but she did experience one or two things herself. She told me over breakfast one morning that she had seen Pepe being silly in her bedroom the night before. I wondered if this really was Pepe or if she was drawing on something she had overheard, so I asked if he was wearing a pointy hat. "No," she answered, "a little round one".

"And was he wearing bright coloured clothes?" I was deliberately misleading.

"No Daddy, just black, but he did have a big red flower."

That was Pepe alright. It appeared he had been doing a spot of babysitting.

She was worried about her spelling test one evening and asked if I could send someone to help her. I told her that Blue Cloud would be there with her. After school the next day she announced with disappointment that she got three out of ten! The next time BC spoke in circle he told Jane indignantly that he managed to live on the earth for one-hundred-and-twenty-four years old without knowing how to spell 'Wednesday'. With hindsight, I probably asked the wrong person for help.

A week or two after we moved in there was a phone call from the tenants who had moved into our old house. "What used to go on in that top room?" Their tone was accusing. "It's haunted or something! We are all too scared to go in there." They were evidently picking up on the powerful atmosphere in the chapel. All I could do was assure them that nothing sinister happened there and that they were perfectly safe.

Word of my work with spirit and the success of the spiritual centre spread nationwide and even overseas. Stairway was selling well and magazine articles published across forty-two countries from New Zealand to Scandinavia brought pilgrims seeking spiritual healing to our door from across the oceans. As healing is often more successful after multiple sessions, our visitors would stay a while in Blue Cloud Lodge before bidding us a fond goodbye, full of enthusiasm for the help they had received. Their word of mouth recommendations resulted in still more international visitors. Albert was happy to be busy, and I was achieving my goal of reaching a wider spectrum of people. Things were going well.

There is no such thing as an incurable disease, only illnesses to which science had not yet discovered the answer. This said, I never guarantee that people will be cured. It is in God's hands. We are not meant to live on

Earth forever. Many people come to us with terminal illnesses. Some leave with a complete, long-lasting cure while others experience some relief although the disease remains. I was, however, hopeful for a long lasting cure for William.

William was a true gentleman. He came to see us with a throat cancer which rendered him unable to speak without the aid of a machine. His devoted wife would bring him from their home in Lancashire to his monthly appointments, and I admit I grew very fond of them both. He was one of many patients, but his beautiful and resilient spirit made him special. What is more, I felt sure we were getting somewhere. The swelling was shrinking, and he was regaining the voice his wife hadn't heard for two years. We were going to beat this.

At that time there was a general hum of excitement in the air from spirit, like I was beginning at last to make some progress with the task I had been given. I took a great deal of satisfaction in that, but my time was increasingly stretched and often I found the enormity of it all overwhelming. Jane did her best to keep me grounded, but with the day to day practicalities of running a hotel, acting as my receptionist and looking after the children her time was limited too. Just over the road, tucked away behind the tram station was Llandudno's oldest pub The King's Head, and I took refuge there when I could, hiding from the problems of the world which I felt squarely on my shoulders.

An Austrian television channel who had read about my work, travelled to Llandudno to make a TV documentary about the strange psychic medium David Drew, Albert Schweitzer and the spirit world. They set up cameras around the hotel and filmed an entire psychic weekend, afterwards interviewing the guests about their experiences. When it aired in Austria, spiritual centres across Europe began to ask if I would attend as a guest speaker. This TV exposure was an exciting opportunity to reach people in countries that I never dreamed I would.

Soon an extensive tour of Scandinavia was arranged, and I found myself flying over the beauty of the Norwegian fjords to embark upon the first leg of a whistle-stop tour of radio stations, spiritual centres and TV studios. Denmark came next with its clinical cleanliness and cuckoo clock houses, then Sweden and the fairy tale feel of Stockholm. Lectures and sittings flew by as countries ran one into another. There was a point when TV cameras filmed me as I spoke on the radio in Denmark. It was madness!

I returned to Blue Cloud Lodge exhausted. Jane had arranged for a two-day respite before my appointments in Llandudno resumed. My head was spinning. After a good night's sleep and some cuddles from the kids, I settled down to sort through the heap of mail which had accumulated while I was travelling.

There were the usual bills which I passed to Jane, some letters from as far afield as Malaysia, New Zealand and Norway asking for consultations, a couple of postal readings (achieved by the wonders of psychometry) and a letter from William's wife on pretty peach note paper. She began by thanking me for all my help, but as I read on, my heart began to break.

William had passed away two weeks earlier.

There followed some of my darkest days. In eighteen years of healing, he was the first terminally ill patient to die on me. Nothing Jane could say would console me. No talk of common sense, the greater good or William's generous and understanding spirit could save me from this feeling of utter desolation. I had abandoned him, and now he was gone. I was so sure that we were getting somewhere. What should I have done? Should I have refused the invitation to speak in Scandinavia? In the vast scheme of things was the passing of one man more or less important than the possibility of rescuing the spiritual welfare of hundreds? Death is not the end so why was I so upset? I knew he was in a better place after all, but the fact remained he came to me for help, and I let him down. The loss of that lovely man will always haunt me.

I often wonder if people think I am untouched by their lives and deaths. Just because I see the infinity of life does not mean I am not moved by a person's parting from this world. I couldn't count the times I have shown someone out after giving messages from their daughter or husband in spirit, knowing that what I said brought them some comfort, but I close the door behind them and weep for their loss just the same. I feel for what they have gone through and for their struggle to live a life without their loved one, at least until it is time for them to meet again in some strange and wonderful land. I constantly feel the weight of their pain upon me, and at times like these it seems the further I carry it the heavier it becomes, but just as steel is forged in fire, the spirit is strengthened by adversity. I know that one day their pain will be behind them and their spirit will be all the better for having experienced it.

10
Giving Up the Ghosts

In many parts of the world, often those which we may regard as uncivilised or primitive, it is a commonplace practice to communicate with one's forefathers. Perhaps these tribes and cultures are more advanced than our arrogance allows us to contemplate.

Those in the spirit world very often try to talk to us. You may not be able to hear their voices, but that doesn't mean that they are not communicating. Spirit can impress thoughts and ideas upon your mind, especially when you are in quiet meditation or a relaxed state. You can experiment with this. Empty your mind of any daily worries, say a little prayer, perhaps play some relaxing music and with practice and patience, you will be amazed at the results. Listen to that inner voice, but remember any decisions or conclusions are yours alone to make.

Communication is not just a one-way street. You can talk to those in spirit just as you would if they were still on the earth. Focus your mind and direct your thoughts to them. They will pick up on this and may even talk back to you. Those on the higher spirit planes find it easiest to communicate. Don't make the mistake of thinking that because I refer to those on certain planes as 'higher', that they are further away. Like radio waves in the air, they are all around us even if we cannot see them. In spirit, there is no such thing as distance or time as we perceive it. We on Earth measure time by the rolling of our planets. In other dimensions, it is quite different. Our years can seem like weeks to them, and distance is no object.

As a general rule, those who recently passed will find it harder to communicate than those who have been in spirit longer, although there are exceptions to this. Someone who has led a very spiritual life for example, will immediately pass to a higher plane where communication may be easier. A husband may pass to spirit, leaving his wife behind, and be reluctant to leave her, holding back his progression. When he does move on he may be surprised to find that communication becomes easier.

Your helpers, as well as your loved ones, like to keep in touch, just as they would if they had emigrated to a faraway country. You have nothing to fear from them, and your family are still the same people that you knew here on Earth, although they may now have a greater understanding if they are learning and progressing well. They want to help you, often seeing things more clearly from where they are, and they will hope to help you to avoid repeating their mistakes.

One way in which it is never wise to try to contact those in spirit, however, is by using the Ouija board. This age-old practice began with an upturned tumbler on a table. Sitters would place their fingers lightly on the glass which would move back and forth without any pressure being applied. Letters and words were arranged on cards around the table, and the pointer would spell out phrases. A well-known toy manufacturer subsequently produced a board-game on the theme, but please, believe me - this is no game!

Do not make the mistake of thinking that those in the spirit world have all the answers. People there, as here, are learning all the time. Just as your loved ones are the same people they always were, this also applies to the evil, misguided and selfish people. Some see the error of their ways and will be helped, but others seek an outlet for their wicked tendencies. Lacking physical bodies to carry out their deeds, they try to attach themselves to people on the earth so they can influence their minds. The Ouija board opens a door which allows them, and anyone else to enter.

You would not dream of going out for the day and leaving your front door open wide. Although you could come home to find that no one had entered, or even that the neighbours had popped over and left you some flowers, it is more likely that burglars and rogues would take advantage of the situation. Now imagine that you return home blindfolded, so you cannot even see who is in the house! Who would dream of placing themselves in such a vulnerable position?

A medium can see who is communicating, but naturally, the average person cannot. This allows evil or unscrupulous spirits to play tricks – or worse! My first personal experience of this came many years ago when a young lady made a desperate call asking for my help. A few weeks earlier she had experimented with the Ouija board in the company of some friends at a party in Lancashire. Since then she had been plagued by strange happenings. The water would suddenly turn off when she was in the shower; lights would turn on without explanation, and she was haunted by the eerie sensation that she was being watched. When she arrived to keep her appointment, a dirty looking character in spirit was one step behind her. He stood over her shoulder, grinning at me as she explained her experiences. Her family were considering psychiatric help, but I could see that her problems were very genuine. This nasty piece of work had formed a link with the girl when she dabbled with the Ouija board, and he was not prepared to let her go without a struggle. With the help of Blue Cloud, we eventually managed to move him on, but he was very persistent. This dreadful situation could so easily have been avoided if she had been warned of the dangers of using the Ouija board.

'Haunting' is the widely understood term for someone in spirit showing themselves at different times in the same vicinity. While frightening to those who experience them, hauntings are usually created by some confused, earthbound but otherwise congenial person in spirit, or 'ghost' as they are more frequently called. Occasionally this is not the case, and some unsavoury being is at the root of the problem.

The word poltergeist originates from the German 'poltern', to create a disturbance and 'geist', which means ghost. It is the term used when someone in spirit is able to have a physical impact on earthly objects by utilising psychic energy. In some, but not all instances, these can even be demonic.

I have often been called out to investigate poltergeist activity which seems to centre on and around an individual adolescent. Youngsters of this age, particularly girls, often generate a lot of psychic energy which can cause objects to move independently. This power of the mind is known as telekinesis and is often confused with spirit activity, although sometimes those in spirit can indeed use this source of energy for their own ends. Either way, the results are alarming and should be taken seriously. While it is true that ghosts cannot physically harm you, in the case of poltergeist activity, a flying object certainly could.

The King's Head in Egremont was a classic example of this. The tenants awoke to find a twelve-inch knife embedded in a kitchen wall. The whitewashed Lake District pub seemed idyllic when the landlord and his wife first arrived, but their hearts sank when they realised that they had taken over one of the most haunted pubs in Britain. Taps would turn themselves on, leaving the floor awash with water, and beer glasses exploded on the bar with some regularity. Ovens would switch themselves on, despite not even being plugged in and the pair awoke one night to hear paper rustling as unseen hands rummaged through their bedroom. At their wits end they put out a nationwide appeal for an exorcist. Maureen read the article in a national paper. She picked up the phone, and offered my services. As the landlord was arranging the meeting, his wife ran into the office calling out that something had burned her chest. She often wore a Celtic cross around her neck, but even though she was not wearing it that day, the outline of the amulet was blistered into her skin.

It was a three-hour drive through rain and sleet from Llandudno to the 18th century rural community pub. The sky was dark when we arrived, and the wind tossed the remnants of last summer's hanging baskets. The bar was humming with local custom, so the landlord took me to one side before describing the frightening experiences which staff and customers had also apparently witnessed. There had been more recent developments. A similar likeness to the Celtic cross but within a kite shape, was found mapped out in salt on the cellar floor. During the previous week a barman became distressed after heavy cellar doors slammed closed, leaving him trapped. On face value it certainly seemed like a genuine case, but I needed to be sure.

I decided to begin with the cellar. The landlord unlocked the thick wooden door for me but chose to stay with the customers in the relative safety of the crowded bar. I steadied myself on the cold stairwell wall and instantly knew that this was no hoax. At the bottom of the steps was a thin, dark-haired but balding man with gaunt face and hollow cheekbones. As he looked through me with cold, deep set eyes, I could tell that he was earthbound and had certainly not found peace on the other side. The pressure of a rope around my neck indicated this man had been hanged. In a flash, the low-ceilinged basement appeared to change into cells, and I concluded that this was more likely an execution than a suicide. No words were exchanged, but he breathed a low moan as he glared at me defiantly. A dirty white shirt was laced at his neck, and his trousers were dark and baggy. Grey mist swirled around his feet. We would have our work cut out with this one. He had obviously been dead for around two hundred years and needed to go into the light, but he could not be forced and probably had no concept of what was happening or how long he had been there.

I closed my eyes and prayed. When I opened them, a bright light had appeared behind the man, and his expression was one of fear - possibly of the unknown. A little time passed before he turned and took that first step towards crossing over, then in an instant, he was gone.

Although I am only five feet seven inches tall, the ceiling down there was so low that I had to stoop as I explored the rest of the cellar. I wanted to be sure that the problem had gone before I reassured the landlord. Glancing around the last corner, I met with another unexpected visitor. A young woman in her thirties stood, hands on hips in an archway. She was oozing attitude. Her blonde hair was loosely tied back, and she wore a long blue dress with puffed sleeves and a low neckline. It was trimmed in what looked like white broderie anglaise. An off-white apron covered most of her skirt, and I immediately recognised that she was the sort of person that displayed a hard shell but had a soft centre. No evil auras here, although she seemed happy to remain earthbound, still putting considerable importance on clothes, jewellery and material possessions. She had passed as the result of a short illness; I estimated around seventy years ago. This serving girl had lived and worked in the hostelry and was not such a dramatic character as the man. Her blue eyes connected with me as she explained with a thought that she was in love with the previous landlord. She also expressed an intense dislike for the landlady, who she mistook for an age-old love rival. I explained that she was misguided and that her actions were not fair on the landlady, who was very frightened by her tricks. I tried to make her understand that she would be so much happier if she let go of earthly things. At first, she was reluctant to show any sensitivity although tears welled in her eyes and she began at last to falter and show some remorse. Suddenly from the shadows appeared two elderly ladies and a man who looked to be around middle age. She fell to her knees as family members reached out their arms, eager to help her understand, to help her over. She had not been able to see them before. Because of her earthbound state, she could only see the world she no longer belonged to, like a snowman in a snow globe, unaware that there was something more beyond her immediate surroundings.

I retired upstairs to the snug. I felt drained, but able to at last reassure the couple that their ghostly residents had moved on. Initially, the landlady was unconvinced. She had previously approached a local vicar for help but he just pooh-poohed the idea. I explained what had happened and her relief that the nightmare was over at last, was palpable. As we spoke her mother and auntie in spirit came to give her proof that this was genuine.

Most vicars are quite naturally unwilling or unable to help when it comes to hauntings and poltergeist activity. They do not understand about life and death, often teaching people that everyone goes directly to heaven when they die. The shifty guy in the cellar was most certainly not in heaven, and was very hesitant to go to his intended destination. The Bible refers to demons being cast out, and to Jesus communicating with Moses and Elijah who had been dead for many years, yet the church is often reluctant to accept such things. I have occasionally been to houses where priests have shaken holy water around in an effort to oust an unwanted presence. I have been called out because it hasn't worked, and has only served to antagonise or amuse the person in spirit, who didn't understand what this strange man was doing in their house. In cases where the ghost is benevolent, it is much easier if someone who can see them simply engages in a chat. Just as if your electrics fail it is better to call an electrician than poke about yourself with what you do not understand, a genuine medium is best qualified to deal with problems regarding those in spirit.

I called a few weeks later to see if all was well, and learned that the tenants had discovered that the King's Head was once a court house with holding cells below for those waiting to be executed.

Coincidentally, my local pub in Llandudno was also called the King's Head. Its boasted claim to fame was as the oldest hostelry in town. With low beams and imposing stone fireplace it certainly looked the part. Little wonder then that the landlord, Juan, encountered some cold spots and strange noises. As we chatted one autumn evening over a pint, he suggested that perhaps I could hold an evening of clairvoyance at the bar. Halloween was approaching, and he proposed that would be the ideal date.

Halloween or All Hallows Eve, is the eve of the Christian festival that remembers the faithful departed. This category includes the saints and martyrs as well as our loved ones. It is believed to have connections with the Celtic harvest festival, whose pagan roots were Christianised by the early church. In many parts of the world, it is observed by attending church and putting flowers and candles on graves. In the United Kingdom and North America, however, it has been corrupted like so many other religious festivals, and is now synonymous with Jack-o-lanterns, horror films and fancy dress parties, the real meaning lost long ago to commercialisation.

On the night of the demonstration, I took a few moments to remind the audience of Halloween's Christian connection before passing on some messages from their own dear departed. Scattered pumpkins flickered and a log fire illuminated the shadowy room, as the Dutch courage flowed.

I often say that I am like a telephone between worlds. That night I was more like a switchboard as messages came in thick and fast. At one point a queue of people in spirit formed beside me as people waited their turn to come through. A little boy of around eight years old appeared in a flash of light, which told me he never saw the light of day, perhaps miscarried, stillborn or aborted eight years ago. In keeping with the season a black cat rubbed around the legs of a woman at the front. Early in the evening, Blue Cloud informed me there were two pregnant ladies in the crowd. The damage had already been done, so to speak, although one of them was not yet aware of it. I announced to the room that I would identify who these ladies were before the evening was out. This gave rise to a few nervous giggles and sideways glances.

By the second half, I had identified one of the women. The girl confirmed that she was indeed expecting, and I advised her to start knitting in pink. As the evening drew to a close, I was disappointed not to have found the other one.

I scanned the crowd, but there were no signs, no clues. I had to draw the evening to a close, having failed to complete the message.

A week or so later I discovered who the pregnant lady was and at last understood why I had not identified her. Psychic gifts are not to be used for the medium's own benefit, and Jane, who had been seated quietly in the corner that Halloween evening, was shocked to find she was expecting our unexpected son, John.

Halloween is no more menacing than any other time of year. In spirit there are good and bad, just like on the earth, and ominous characters can make their presence felt at any time. Perhaps the most sinister entity I encountered was in a Liverpool club owned by actor Ricky Tomlinson. It was after the 'Brookside' days, but before his big breaks in TV's 'The Royle Family' and 'Cracker'. He was running a casting agency at that time and a club called 'The Limelight'. As a result of an article in the Liverpool Echo about strange happenings and poltergeist activity at the club, Maureen phoned Ricky to ask if he would like my help.

The article told how a friend and regular at the club who was visiting Ricky became unwell and went upstairs to lie down. She was a battle hardened lady who had suffered and survived on the streets of Liverpool for many years. She was afraid of nothing and would hold her own against any man. A few moments after she went upstairs, Ricky heard a crash and the most dreadful scream. When he ran into the room, she was outside, teetering on a narrow ornamental balcony four stories above the street below. She had smashed the window with a chair and was now clinging to the edge, petrified. Whatever she had seen in the room was obviously more frightening to her than the risk of plunging to her death on the pavement. Ricky pulled her inside and with trembling voice she explained that a 'big fella' appeared at the door and wouldn't let her out. He was bald with a long coat, and he told her he was waiting for Nellie. There was no logical explanation for this man's appearance or indeed disappearance. Two days later a regular patron of the club passed away suddenly. Her name was Nellie.

A decorative spiral staircase ascended from the lobby to the casting agency on the first floor. Above it was the club and upwards again was some modest accommodation. One afternoon on his way to the gents, Ricky passed a young lady on the landing. She had a baby in a pram and a toddler at her side. He said 'Hello' and carried on down the stairs before realising that there was no way the woman could get down that staircase with a pram without help. When he turned back to help her she had mysteriously gone. He ran down about fifteen steps to the street below, but she was nowhere in sight.

The following morning Ricky mentioned this to a mechanic who occupied one of the top rooms. The man didn't appear surprised, but he did seem disturbed. He explained that he had taken to turning his face to the wall every morning when he came down the stairs. This was because when he looked over the bannister, he would often see a woman with a pram going down the stairs, but when he reached the front door it was always locked, and the woman was nowhere to be seen.

Other weird happenings included lights turning off and pool balls behaving strangely. On one occasion when he was clearing glasses, Ricky heard voices coming from another upstairs room. Some friends who had stayed behind for a drink after hours, crept upstairs to listen, and they all confirmed that there were voices. A bank operated from the ground floor of the building, and there had been a previous attempt to break in via the upper floors, so assuming a similar incident was taking place, they called the police. Four officers arrived and heard the voices coming from the locked room. Ricky quietly turned the key then flung the door open. There was no one there. There was little doubt that this was genuine.

The first time we first pulled up outside the tall, blackened brick building, it looked almost derelict. Upon entering however, I could feel it was alive with spirit. The eerie ambience immediately indicated there was someone here who was up to no good. We climbed the stairs to the bar where Ricky was waiting to welcome us. The first thing that struck me about this strapping scouser was that he didn't seem the type to scare easily. We chatted over a pint as I listened to his account of the problems they had been having. His manner was warm and friendly, but he was clearly concerned. There were a few patrons in the club, so I decided the best approach might be to return one night and venture through the building alone, to see if anyone made contact.

It took a few days to address the different characters there. The backdrop to my third visit was weather fit for any classic horror film. As rain teamed down and thunder rolled across the black sky, I shook my umbrella and went inside. Ricky greeted me with a pint, then waited in the bar as I wandered off alone through the building. The atmosphere was oppressive, like I was descending into the pits. There was a tangible air of foreboding. My hand slid up the icy bannister as I spiralled my way from floor to floor, entering random disused rooms and dodging the rain which dripped periodically through sodden ceilings onto bare boards. The pungent odour seemed to grow stronger, and I realised that I could easily get lost in this maze of rooms and corridors. I turned left into a large abandoned bathroom. Dead end. It was as I turned to leave that I saw him in the doorway. It was the bald man in the long dark coat. He appeared to be over six feet tall and of powerful build. A tremulous shout erupted from him as through glazed eyes he fixed me with a menacing stare. The lilt was Irish. "Wait 'till I get my hands on him! I'm going to kill him!"

I stopped short, his sudden appearance taking me by surprise, then before I could react empty bleach and shampoo bottles came flying at me from his direction. Instinctively I raised my hands to shield my face, and when the barrage ended, I saw another smaller man in the shadows to my right. He was unkempt and unshaven. Long, greasy hair fell across his face, and he was incredibly agitated. In a split second, I was shown the scenario. The scrawny little guy had murdered the bald man with a sawn-off shotgun in some gangland type confrontation many years ago when the building housed a gentlemen's club. He had then turned the gun on himself. It had a feel of the 1970's, but the feud was still going on in the afterlife, morphing the atmosphere and creating conditions which allowed two worlds to intermingle, like an open door.

The hatred between these two characters was palpable, like an electric field, and it seemed Blue Cloud and his friends in high spirit were not about to take any more chances with my safety. The air began to swirl around us and all at once a loud swoosh and a beam of brilliant light whisked the sinister pair away. They had been moved on to their rightful homes in the spirit world, where they would have perhaps hundreds of earthly years to come to terms with the consequences of their lifestyles. Whether they continued to do the work of the devil or changed their ways and repented would be up to them. I stood for a moment or two in the sudden calm of the dingy bathroom, waiting for my eyes to adjust to the half-light and listening to the storm outside.

On my way downstairs, I felt a little light headed and tremendously thankful for my good friend Blue Cloud's help. Ricky said I looked awful, but I assured him that the problem should now be resolved. We had a few pints and exchanged a few jokes, relieved that it was over. When I mentioned my public demonstrations, it gave him an idea. He invited me to hold an evening of clairvoyance there in The Limelight, for some of his friends and colleagues.

We agreed a date for a few weeks later, and I decided to theme the evening around psychometry, taking items from the audience and sharing the information I received by holding them. Ideally, the object should be something the owner has had for a long time, perhaps an item of jewellery or something they frequently use, as opposed to a bus ticket, which I was once presented with but from which I could pick up very little. Alternatively, it can be something that belonged to someone who is now in spirit. Either way, the fewer people that touch it the better, as this can create some confusion, like a crossed wire.

Ricky decided to record the evening, and I arrived twenty minutes early to find the club filled with actors, film extras and Ricky's friends and acquaintances. As with any evening of clairvoyance, I don't know who is going to be there on either side of the veil. Those in spirit take the trouble to be there, just like the audience does, but I can't call anyone up. In the past I have been put under pressure with questions like, 'can you ask my granddad if the money was meant to be mine', but if he isn't there, I can't ask him anything.

The atmosphere that night was casual and relaxed. Ricky began the evening with a short account of the supernatural experiences he had encountered at the club, and why he had asked for my help.

"I asked David if there was anyone there, and he said, 'Yes, there is!'

I always thought that ghosts were de-frocked vicars from the eighteenth century, or nuns that had been caught doing things other than their holy duties." This raised a giggle. *"David said there was a tall, Irish man - which was exactly what Chloe had told me, which he knew nothing about - and a young guy who had committed a murder and then committed suicide. This in itself was fascinating enough, but more importantly a friend of mine walked into the room as David was sitting there. They had never met each other before. I introduced them and he said he was sorry to hear about her tummy trouble, but that she was not to worry. She explained that she didn't have any tummy trouble. Since that night she has learned that she has got to have laser treatment on a complaint to her tummy.*

This is not made up, I am not a 'Tom Pepper'. Ninety percent of the people in this room know me and I hope trust me. I implicitly trust this man who is about to come up and speak. I don't know what he is going to do, but I am delighted to know him."

With that I stood up and made a start. Everyone seemed to enjoy the psychometry. There were a few humorous moments, although some people inevitably left in tears. Footage of the evening found its way onto 'YouTube' in the years that followed and it remains there today.

Ricky and I kept in touch. He introduced me onto the stage when I held an evening of clairvoyance at Preston Guild Hall, and he joined me for several charity events, including a show for BBC Children in need at Southport's Floral Hall. Ricky has always been enthusiastic when helping charitable causes, but he had no idea at that time that he would soon be in need of charity himself.

When people come to me for a personal reading, it is not always to seek comfort in contacting a loved one. Sometimes they are looking for guidance from those who can perhaps see their pathway more clearly. The Limelight club, which Ricky had invested in after quitting 'Brookside' following a row with producers, went bust, leaving him all but destitute. Jobless and broke he considered turning his back on acting and going back to his original trade as a builder. Unsure where life was taking him, he came to me with an open mind for some career advice and a little guidance. I examined the signs and symbols in his aura, and could see that there were various pathways before him. I told him that 'Brookside' had been a stepping stone to greater things and that if he concentrated on acting he would be back on television doing bigger and better things, but first he would have to navigate a very dark period. Ricky decided to stick with it and weather the storm. His relationship failed, and he hit rock bottom, but then opportunities began to present themselves, and he went from strength to strength. Soon he was starring in such outstanding dramas as 'Cracker', 'Playing the Field', 'Riff Raff', 'Roughnecks' and of course the hilarious hit comedy show, 'The Royle Family'. He married happily, and his life turned a well-deserved corner. His autobiography, 'Ricky', includes a section about the ghosts in the Limelight club, and how he and I came to meet.

When I take a moment to recall, I remember giving readings in some weird and wonderful places. It all started in my mum's front room, then my own living room and subsequently my office, but I have also been cornered in the supermarket and pub by acquaintances needing advice. To be honest, if a stranger asks what I do for a living, I often say I am a bus driver, just to avoid psychic phenomena being the conversation for the night. I even gave three nurses readings in the laundry room of a hospital once! It was during the Llandudno floods of 1993. I had returned home to find the lower floor of Blue Cloud Lodge under water. Amidst all the panic and confusion I collapsed with a heart attack and was rushed to Llandudno Hospital. It was my second night on the ward when I awoke to find a nurse leaning over me in the half-light asking if I could see anything with her. My reputation had preceded me. There was one thing I was desperate for, and if she wanted a reading, it was going to cost her. "I can't do anything without a cigarette."

Before I knew it, three nurses were wheeling my bed into the laundry room where they opened the windows. I took my time telling them all what I saw, as I dragged the smoke up from by toes, savouring every puff.

There was another peculiar occasion where I gave readings to six people picked at random from Llandudno promenade on a summer's afternoon. A reporter from 'Take a Break, Fate and Fortune' magazine was running a series of articles entitled 'Psychic Roadshow', designed to test the powers of various psychics. Bizarrely she took me to the sea front, parked me by some railings and selected six strangers to bring to me one by one. Afterwards, she interviewed them to see if what I told them rang true. It was a very odd experience.

The article was a double page spread entitled 'How did he know that?' They concluded it by running a competition whereby readers could win the chance to have a private reading with me. This is how it went.

The first lady was a twenty-two-year-old full-time mum.

David: "Interference from family has caused a rift with your partner – he listens too much to others. A female with the initial C or K is stirring things up. I see a move in ten months and a baby next year. Finances are a problem, and they are causing friction – maybe you fell out with someone this morning? Someone recently offered you a chance to make money, but you didn't take it. If you had it would have led to new opportunities and by the end of the year your money worries could have been over."

Response: "I can't believe it! I split up with my boyfriend this morning after a row. And he listens to rumours about me. His family don't like me and mine don't like him, so there has always been trouble. I have a friend whose name begins with the letter K and I suspect she isn't doing me any favours. I was asked to become a lap dancer but turned it down. Maybe I was a bit hasty!"

The second lady was a thirty-two-year-old postwoman.

David: "There is an opportunity coming up, but you lack confidence. I can see an important document concerning solicitors that will need your signature, and a house move or a change of surroundings. In spirit, there is an Anna or Annie. There are three big celebrations on the horizon: something in August, a special celebration in November or December, and you will be toasting something important next Easter."

Response: "David is right about my confidence – I do tend to hold back. My boyfriend wants us to move although I am not so keen. I had a great-grandmother called Annie, but she died before I was born. I am going to a wedding in November, although nothing is planned for August – but I'll wait for my invite now. Now that David has mentioned a celebration next Easter, I'm hoping that my boyfriend will pop the question."

The next lady was a thirty-year-old full-time mum.

David: "You are coming to the point where you don't know who you can turn to for help. Changes are afoot. You will live somewhere different and make a new circle of friends. Everyone comes to you with their problems, so you should consider going into nursing, counselling or teaching. You are worrying about the health of three people. One, who is older than you, can't walk very well. The other two are a boy and a girl.

Response: "I am shaking because David was so accurate. I worry about my dad who had a shattered leg after being hit by a car. My son had a broken arm which isn't healing well, and my daughter suffers from congenital heart disease. Spookily, I've been looking into the careers David mentioned. My husband is looking for a new job – could be that complete change David mentioned?"

The next lady was a fourty-four-year-old retail manager.

David: "You are someone who gives the impression of being relaxed and calm on the outside, but the inner you worries constantly. I see a major decision being made within the next two months and your life will change as a result. You are waiting for someone else to make the first move, but you should act first. Family and friends may influence you, but it is your decision. There is a house move – either yours or you will be helping someone else.

Despite a lot of stress, things will work out, so don't be nervous about making that decision."

Response: "He's right about me being calm on the outside. I'm terrible for worrying late at night or early in the morning. I am highly strung inside, and my family does discuss things openly. Everyone has a say, but if I really want something I always do things my way."

The next lady was a thirty-nine-year-old office worker.

David: "Someone is very stubborn, and it is hard to get them to see things your way. Three years ago things were very stressful, but you are much happier now. I get the feeling that you have moved recently. I see sparks flying so check your wiring. You have recently fallen out with someone and need to start thinking about a reconciliation. Is 21st of September significant?

Response: "The stubborn person is my fourteen-year-old daughter. We do have battles of wills, but that is teenagers for you. I've married someone in the last three years and we are really happy. We have just moved into an old house, so I'll keep an eye on the electrics. I have fallen out with someone but I'm not sure about a reconciliation. If my dad were still alive his birthday would have been on 22nd September – so David was only one day out."

The final lady was a thirty-eight-year-old full-time mum.

David: "You are having major alterations done in your home – I see you surrounded by quite a bit of rubble. In terms of spirit, there is a lady whose name begins with the letter M and a baby boy who was lost about a year ago. Someone has a problem with their left leg – perhaps it is something to do with their hip, – and you'll go with them to hospital. A significant birthday is coming up on the 4th or 14th of the month. Expect to have a baby boy later this year."

Response: "That was totally unbelievable! I am pregnant, although I am not showing, and I miscarried a little boy last year. The lady in spirit is Margaret, my 'second mum'. The rubble is due to the kitchen extension we are having built – the mess is driving me crazy! My mum has a bad hip and I am due to go to the hospital with her."

When I give a reading, it is derived from a combination of what spirit are telling me and what they show me within the aura. Sometimes it is very clear, but at other times words are harder to catch, symbols more complicated to interpret. In these cases, it can be a puzzle working out what they are trying to get across. Blue Cloud and the gang work very hard to help them communicate.

The same is true in the case of public demonstrations of clairvoyance and clairaudience. Many people are made busy in helping the person in spirit to get their message across, especially if their passing was recent or traumatic.

I recall two young ladies who turned out to be sisters, sitting in the front row of one of my Llandudno demonstrations. Immediately a young man was beside me. I pointed to one of the girls. "Whoa, I fancy her on the front row!" The words were out of my mouth before I had time to re-phrase. The girl looked a little alarmed. I explained that this young man in spirit still fancied her. She replied in a Liverpool accent, "I should think so too!" Everyone laughed. I could see him standing beside her now as he placed a bouquet of red roses on her lap. She explained that it was her boyfriend Gary, who always bought her red roses. A voice in my ear told me he lost a shoe. The girl looked surprised by this and asked me to describe it. I was shown a white trainer with green stripes. She confirmed that he did own trainers like these but was not aware he had lost one. Next, I was shown a stone coloured shirt with a motif of a man. She explained this was his favourite shirt. "I was wearing it when I died." The voice said.

I asked the girl's name, Lana, before relaying this part of the message. She didn't know if it was true as she didn't see him on the day he died. Emotional now, he told me to tell her that he was sorry, she was right about there being a place you go when you die, he had been wrong, and that she shouldn't worry about the mix up at the funeral because he wasn't there anyway. Lana confirmed that although she believed in an afterlife, her boyfriend didn't, and that due to some miscommunication she almost missed the beginning of his funeral. This had devastated her and played on her mind afterwards.

I went on to tell Lana that Gary had been in shock after he passed, and he was still somewhat earthbound. He was reluctant to leave her and was still in love with her. He told me he still shared her bed. She gasped, putting her hand to her mouth. It seems she had felt him lying next to her, comforting her at night. He said he had been busy and was building a home over there.

As the message began to fade, I felt a crushing sensation in my chest, like I couldn't breathe. I asked Lana how Gary died, and she told me it was asphyxiation. Gary's voice sounded sad now. "I shouldn't have been there. I was in the wrong place at the ground." I passed the message on word for word as I didn't understand what he meant. Lana explained that he had died in the crush of the Hillsborough disaster, at the semi-final of Liverpool FC and Nottingham Forrest on 15th April 1989. He shouldn't have been in the terraces, but he swapped his ticket with an older gentleman in their group so that the man could sit down - a seemingly insignificant act that changed the course of many lives.

The next message of the evening was for Lana's sister Angie, who sat beside her. "Who is Paddy?" I asked. It was her uncle. "He's alive." She added. Obviously, this must be for someone else, a crossed wire perhaps, so I moved on.

A young girl of around eighteen suddenly stood beside me. She whispered her name was Nicola and that she died of leukaemia. Angie recognised who she was. Nicola was desperate to pass a message on to her mum to let her know she was often around her, especially in the family home. As her mother was not present she wanted to send her proof somehow. She told me that Angie had a watch in her bedroom drawer, hidden among her underwear and that it had stopped at 9.40. She explained that when Angie went home to Liverpool and found that this was true she would know the message was genuine and would be able to tell her mum that she was alright.

I was distracted by a lady with glass of wine in hand, out for a girly night with her friend.

"I have a young man here." He was quite pushy and I found myself responding to him out loud. "*Yes, I am trying to explain!*"

"He wants you to know," "*Yes, I'm telling her.*" "His name is David." "*Yes, hang on!*" "He was on a bike." "*Was it a motorbike?*" "No, a push-bike. You called him something else. You called him 'Ditchy'. He wants you to know it was him that night." "*Yes, I'm telling her now.*" "He wanted to frighten you because of the fire. Does this make sense?"

The lady was called Joanne, and the words I spoke 'knocked the wind out of her', as she put it. When she was in her teens she would hang around with a group of friends, one being a lad called David. One afternoon he was riding his bike down a hill when the brakes failed. He went under a lorry and was killed instantly. His pals were heartbroken.

Around ten years later Joanne was staying overnight with a friend as they planned a trip to Wales the next morning. She awoke at 2 a.m. with the feeling that something was not quite right. Slowly opening her eyes she saw the silhouette of a man leaning over the bed. Thinking this was an intruder she kept her eyes narrow so the whites of her eyes would not betray her. After about thirty seconds he turned and walked toward the window, concealing himself behind the curtain. Joanne pushed her friend to wake her, whispering, "There's a man behind the curtain!" When they turned on the light there was no-one there.

Joanne and her friend stayed awake until the next day when it was time to leave. When they returned from their trip they were in for a shock. A woman in the apartment directly below where they had been sleeping had started a fire which tore through the building. Joanne's friend lost everything, but at least they were safe.

A week or so after the demonstration I had news from the sisters. Angie had found a watch belonging to an ex-boyfriend in her underwear drawer. She had no idea it was there. It had stopped at 9.40. Nicola's auntie lived next-door-but-one to Angie. She cried when she told her about the message, and hurried round to pass it on to her mum.

Lana had since seen footage of the Hillsborough disaster and could pick Gary out of the crowd. He was wearing his favourite stone coloured shirt. A friend who was with him that day told her that he was found wearing only one shoe.

They added that Uncle Paddy, who they thought was alive, passed away unexpectedly on the night of the demonstration.

11
Mysteries and Miracles

Years at Blue Cloud Lodge passed happily. Campanula grew like purple lace through the garden, and contentment radiated from its walls. The summers were busy for the hotel, and B.A.S.E was thriving. The winters were cosy, more relaxing but less profitable. We drained the last drops of the season and appreciated the change of pace when it came.

The spring of 1998 came upon us suddenly. I recall the blooms of cherry blossom trees which lined the street, appeared one morning quite unannounced, scattering pink confetti where it seemed only a moment ago, crisp, amber leaves swirled. The tramway awoke from its hibernation to the rumble of cable testing, while the ticket office and gift shop staff dusted off their postcards, kites and fridge magnets ready for the Easter rush. Winter had moved on at last.

At three-thirty on the morning of Good Friday, I was awakened by the suggestion of a telephone ringing in the distance. I fumbled, eyes closed for the receiver. It was the theatre sister from a hospital in Kettering. My senses gathered as she told me that Maureen had been involved in a horrific car accident on the A14, and she was not expected to survive. As she was being wheeled to the operating theatre, she deliriously asked a nurse to phone me and explain what had happened. They were about to take her into surgery with the intention of amputating her feet. My response must have seemed strange. "Please ask them not to amputate. Tell her I will be in there with her." I went into my office to meditate and pray.

Later I learned that her car had hit the back of a slow moving articulated lorry in torrential rain. The impact pushed the engine through into the cabin of her car. She had multiple injuries to her shoulders, ribs and legs, but worst of all her feet were facing the wrong way, hanging by a thread.

Maureen remained unconscious, heavily sedated for six days. On the seventh, she was visited by a lower limb specialist, who told her she must surely be the luckiest person alive. He said he had dealt with many cases like this throughout his career, and had seen feet with forty percent fewer injuries that he had been unable to salvage. "How I managed to save yours I do not know!" he added.

She was unashamed to notify him that she had asked me for spiritual healing, and she went on to tell him about my work. He nodded as he took it all in.

"Will you thank him for me?" He said, "I come from a spiritual nation and I believe what you are saying."

Maureen was ultimately able to keep her feet, although doctors told her she would never walk again. They were wrong. After a period of rehabilitation, she was back to running around like the whirlwind she always was.

Miracles are all around us, and angels do exist. God's ministering angels bridge the gap between God and man, between heaven and all the other planes. They do the will of God, fulfil his errands, just as on the other side of the coin demons do the work of the devil.

You will read about angel sightings, and these can be very real, although often people mistake their guides or other high spirit beings for angels. I very often see them, sometimes in the middle of the night when I least expect it. Not everyone who dwells in heaven is an angel, however. They are the highest of the high. Some have never walked the earth, but others have experienced earthly lives themselves, which demonstrates that anyone can strive over the ages to become an angel.

Blue Cloud always says that everything happens for a purpose. Every new location which life led me to, introduced me to people I would otherwise never have met, people whose lives I have endeavoured to influence for the better in the hope that they might avoid stumbling blindly into the pits. It is my reason for being, but if I stood on a box or shouted from the rooftops in this day and age no one would listen. They might send for the men in white coats, and if not, at the very least my words would carry little weight. We influence or we are influenced. I try to do this subtly in everyday life. There is a time and a place for grand statements, so I try to quietly inspire whenever I can.

If you lead a good life, there is no reason to fear death. The secret is to recognise the strands of evil that are hidden in the actions of people around us, and not to imitate them. The next step is to be ambitious, not in your career (although there is nothing wrong with that), but in your spirituality. You will make mistakes but be as good as you can be. You know in your heart the right thing to do. Just pray for the strength to do it.

After fifteen happy years, it became evident it was time to leave Blue Cloud Lodge and seek out new environments. All things have their purpose and their time. While my work thrived, it was mostly non-profit making and the hotel, which was quiet in the winter and occupied much of

Jane's time, was struggling to break even. Once more my hand was being forced to make a change.

We invested in a small pub in Llandudno, which Ricky kindly opened for us, and we ran the hotel alongside it for a while, but my work suffered, and it became increasingly apparent that we needed to re-think.

Selling the Llandudno businesses, we bought an oak beamed pub in historic Chester, a pretty, walled city which began life as a Roman fort. It boasts numerous medieval buildings, although many of the black and white shops and houses within the walls were restored by the Victorians. The pub was a listed building not far from the magnificent cathedral and the famous Eastgate clock. Aptly it was a feature of the 'Haunted Chester Tour', described as one of the most haunted buildings in the city centre. No concerns there for the Drew family.

The signage spelt 'Marlbor**or**ough Arms', the story being that the sign writer took a break half way through his work and became flustered after seeing an apparition at the bedroom window, hastily finishing the sign but losing his concentration and adding an extra 'OR' to the word. The new spelling had stuck and subsequently became a famous oddity in Chester.

Around one hundred years ago, a previous landlord committed suicide in the cellar rather than face debtor's prison. He leant across a barrel, and slit his throat. As I skipped down the steps to change a barrel, I would often hear him whisper, "David". I was usually too busy to stay and chat, but it was clear he was proud of his real ales and reluctant to entirely hand over their care to someone else. The previous landlady warned us that barrels could often be heard rolling around the cellar in the early hours of the morning. Sure enough at twenty-past-four every morning, bangs and rumbles from down below would disturb the family's sleep.

In the gent's toilet at the rear of the building, the spirit of a local stable hand introduced himself to me after closing time one evening as Gilbert. He was bald on top, but his grey hair was quite long around the back and sides. His eyes were dark and deep set with bags underneath, but he was friendly and quite chatty. He would often appear there in his herringbone coat to say hello at the end of a busy day. I presume the toilets had been built where the stables used to be.

Upstairs in the living quarters, more ghostly lodgers made their presence known. One joker would imitate our voices. He would shout Ayesha in my voice, or Sian in Ayesha's voice. When they came running, of course, there was no one there. One afternoon Jane heard a child crying loudly. She dropped what she was doing and ran down the corridor, thinking it was John in some distress. She came to an abrupt stop in front of the open bathroom door where the sound was loudest. The sobbing was right beside her, but there was no one there. A few days later Ayesha saw a young boy in cream clothing watching her from a staircase in the same area.

Early one Sunday morning before the pub was open, John who was around seven years old, saw a man in a black suit standing at the end of the bar, in front of the fireplace, where a long since broken mantle clock would occasionally strike. At first, he thought it was a customer, but then he realised the pub was closed. When he told me what he had seen, I checked the CCTV. It recorded him doing a double take before backing out of the bar, eyes fixed on the fireplace where a blurry spot hovered on camera.

Richard Felix, presenter of TV's Most Haunted, heard I had taken over the Marlbororough and approached me for an interview regarding the ghostly happenings. It was to be shown in a DVD production called 'Cheshire Ghosts'. The building was notorious for strange happenings, and I suppose a spiritual medium taking over the pub only added to the interest.

None of our spirit tenants were a problem to us, and they seemed quite happy just as they were for the time being. The offer to help them move on was there if they wished to take me up on it, but none applied. They were rather attached to the place, and I suspect they are still there to this day.

Running a city centre pub guarantees a steady flow of new faces among the stalwart regulars. I was determined to make the Marlborough a nice pub for nice people, a place where everyone felt safe, and a lady could call in for a coffee without feeling uncomfortable. We hired doorman at the weekends to discourage trouble, and soon we had a faithful clientele who we regarded more as friends than customers. Where we encountered racist or cruel behaviour, I tried to show there was a better way to live. Locals would often feel they could approach me for a favour if they were in need, and I was proud that they felt that way. Some could not understand why I seemed so willing to put myself out for other people, but I didn't allow their cynicism to deter me, despite the strange looks.

Standing behind the bar is a marvellous place for observing people and communicating with them. Barmen and barmaids across the country listen to customers unburden themselves of their worries. In a way they are the unsung counsellors. People from all walks of life forget their problems over a pint. Each afternoon, solicitors, road-sweepers, bank managers and postmen would gather in the pub and chat together on a level playing field. I loved that.

This is how things should be throughout the world. Whether you are a brain surgeon or a refuse collector, you should be the best you can be at what you do and look upon each person as an equal.

One afternoon a thirty-something lady came in, propping her shopping bags against the bar as she ordered an espresso. I passed her the coffee, and as she slipped the change into my hand, a flash of recognition crossed her face.

"David Drew!" she shrieked, "What are you doing here?"

I explained that I had bought the pub and tried not to make it obvious that I had no idea who she was. I failed.

"You remember me, don't you? I used to bring my mum to see you."

I smiled blankly as my eyes desperately searched her face for a clue.

"She always wore a green coat with a brooch."

"Oh yes," I relaxed as the penny began to drop, "I can see her now!"

She looked horrified. "No, no. She's not dead!"

We had a chuckle as I tried to explain that it was just a figure of speech.

Other pub landlords in the city kept themselves to themselves and seemed to look upon each other as nothing more than business rivals. I started to walk around different bars on a Thursday night and chat to the other landlords. Soon the idea caught on, and they began to meet on a regular basis, walking around the city pubs, united over shared ideas, a pint and a joke or two.

The week before Christmas in 2005, it was reported that a mother in nearby Saltney was left devastated when thieves broke into their home and stole all her children's presents. Police appealed for information, and I was deeply moved when I read the story. It reminded me of my mum and her struggle to make our Christmas' happy. I had to do something. In the spirit of Christmas, I took £400 from the rent money and sent it to the family with my best wishes. A few days later the young lady came into the Marlborough to thank me. She fought back tears as she spoke of how rare it is to find good hearted people these days. It was a sobering thought. I explained that seeing her face and knowing the children would not go without on Christmas morning, was thanks enough.

Some locals who were in the pub waited until she left, and then began to jeer at me, "Well, we could all do that if we had your money!"

I was saddened by the remarks, but resisted telling them that I would be short on the rent that month and that they were in all probability better off than I was. Jane and I economised on Christmas that year and were happy to do it.

The pressure that parents feel at Christmas is becoming more intense year on year. Thanks to advertising and corporate greed, children are expecting more and more. The symbolic giving of a present to commemorate the shepherd's gifts to Jesus has turned into an avaricious industry that we have all bought in to. How can anyone deny their children when they, in all innocence, expect so much? The little ones couldn't possibly understand the reality of the pressure this creates, or that the single mum or out of work dad is placed in an impossible position. We all want to see our children happy on Christmas morning, and not everyone has someone as wonderful as my mother's milkman to help out.

Every action is returned to us either in this world or the next. What we have visited on other people, good or bad is returned to us. In India they call this karma; Christians say, 'As ye sow, so shall ye reap.' This perfect balance is part of God's natural laws.

I have heard people say there is no justice in the world, but ultimately there is, or at least if not in this world, in the next. This is why revenge is pointless. If you retaliate with a wicked act, then your actions will be revisited on you in time, just as theirs will. We are not to decide when. Good or bad, your actions do not pass unnoticed, and all are paid back for them, like for like.

We cannot always repay someone personally for what they did, but we can remember their actions and do the same for another when the opportunity presents itself.

I wanted to pay the milkman's kindness forward, to pass on the compassion he showed us to others and let it grow.

When we were living in Blue Cloud Lodge, Jane and I decided in the spirit of the season to take a leaf out of his book. We set up a collection to help out needy families with presents for their children. We called it 'Scarlet Ribbons', like the song in which a father hears his daughter praying for some red ribbons, but is unable to get any for her as the shops are all closed. He retires, upset at his failure, but when he awakens mysterious scarlet ribbons have appeared at the foot of his daughter's bed.

The local papers were kind enough to publicise our appeal for donations, and Jane approached the shops in town, hoping for some small offerings. The results were disappointing. Only a few kind individuals were prepared to give, and hardly any businesses were interested in the cause. There were not enough people giving and far too many needing. We provided most of the toys for the families who applied ourselves. A sad defeat for the spirit of Christmas vs. the indifference of man.

You may have noticed that every year there are fewer religious themed cards in circulation in the UK. They are dwindling from the shops, and it saddens me at heart. Christmas is not about robins, holly and puddings, it is the time we choose to remember that God sent His Son from the safety of His arms to a world where he would suffer at the hands of the spiritually ignorant. It was His gift to everyone here - the hope that they might be saved from the horrors of hell. All they had to do was learn from his teachings. How does a card with a robin remind us of that?

Last December Maureen approached the manager of WH Smith to ask why there were no religious cards on the shelves. He told her that it was for fear of upsetting religious minorities. Surely we should all be able to celebrate our diverse religious festivals equally? No one is forced to celebrate Christmas, but those who want to should be free to do so in a manner which reflects its meaning, and we should not be afraid or ashamed. We live in a time where people flinch more if you quietly mention God than they would if you shouted some obscenity. This is so sad, and it must change, or we are lost.

In the spirit world, Christmas has not been corrupted. Those who choose to celebrate the birth of Christ have no distractions, no drunken staff parties, no credit card bills and no supermarket queues. The most affluent societies are usually the most spiritually bankrupt. As we choose to remember Christmas on December 25th, our loved ones in spirit see us putting up the tree and the decorations, and they want to be with us as we celebrate. Those who are high find it easy to visit, those who are not are helped and advised on how to do it. From where they are they can see the folly that has consumed us, and it saddens them. Few people on the earth today recognise the true meaning of the season, and those who have passed over tend to be filled with regret, vowing if they had another life they would do things differently.

As Christmas Eve turns to Christmas Day and the faithful worship at midnight mass, in spirit those who wish it are given a very special opportunity. The spirit of Christ travels through all the planes. The Christ Spirit has been in existence since the beginning of time. Two thousand years ago He had a life on Earth in a physical body in accordance with God's natural laws, to spread a very important message and heal the sick. He was born to Mary and Joseph, and they called Him Jesus. Christmas is a sacred time when people celebrate His birth and give thanks.

On the high spirit planes, He will be seen very clearly as He makes himself available to everyone at Christmas, and all people of every plane are given the chance to see Him. In the dark, murky pits He may appear as a shining light, but what is obvious to one may not be so to another. Some are not interested; others become remorseful. Some people do not recognise what is before them. The Christ Spirit is a part of God, and when He is near, angels sing praises to God in the highest. They try to help people, here as well as there, to understand the true meaning of Christmas.

Those in spirit whose beliefs do not involve Christ, may not be interested or may not understand this phenomenon. Some Christians think that Jesus was God, others that He was just a prophet. Everyone is entitled to their beliefs, but there is only one truth regardless of what people believe, and all have the opportunity to understand that the Christ Spirit does exist. God is the unchanging constant in all of this. There is no religion, and there are no wars in spirit. The truth is simply the truth.

When my son John was eighteen months old, Jane took him outside in his pyjamas on Christmas Eve to look for Santa on his sleigh. It was the first Christmas that he had been old enough to participate in, and we had not yet taught him the story of the Nativity. She picked him up in the cold night air and looking upward asked him, "What can you see?"

He pointed to the sky, eyes bright and said a word no-one had ever taught him, "Angels!"

Jane fell quiet, and with a lump in her throat strained her eyes, hoping to see what he was seeing. If only we didn't lose the innocence and clarity of infancy.

12
Calling Time

We adapted to city life as best we could and encountered some fascinating characters during our Chester years - on both sides of the veil! Some of the customers turned out to be more troublesome and scary than the spirits who haunted the place, but others like gold nuggets in a pan of silt and gravel came to be dear friends. Our time here highlighted more than ever the fact that intellect is not directly proportional to spirituality. One erudite and well-spoken customer of dubious integrity, admitted one afternoon over a pint of London Pride, to having stared into a mirror and offered his soul to the devil if only his girlfriend would come back to him - which she did, although only for a little while. He perhaps should have asked about the small print! For anyone to contemplate such a bargain, I suspect he was on course for the pits in any case. Another stocky character with shaven head and Union Jack tattoo, bragged without shame one rainy afternoon that he had claimed as his own £2,000 in twenty-pound notes, which he found on the historic Chester rows, rolled up and secured with a rubber band. When I asked why he didn't hand it in to the police, he looked at me with a blank expression and went on to tell me in detail how he had spent it. He could not have cared less that someone must have been distraught at losing such a significant amount of money.

There has always been some mild rivalry between Wales and England, as is often the case in any borderlands. When Wrexham football club met with Chester, you could count on trouble in the city centre, and sensible locals stayed home until the rival fans dispersed. Even Chester Town Hall clock, which should have worn a face on all four sides of its square turret, had only three dials. The side that faced towards Wales was left deliberately blank so as not to give the Welsh the time of day. The locals take pleasure in saying that there is to this day a law which was never repealed stating it is legal to shoot a Welshman with a bow and arrow if he is seen within the walls of Chester after midnight. Luckily I wasn't one to go out much after dark.

The day came when our days in the city of Chester had run their course and in my heart I felt it was time for the family to move back to Wales. The yearning to go home only intensified. In truth, our hearts had never left.

Planning the great escape, we bought a family home in Llandudno, then sold the Marlborough Arms to a young man who promised he would keep it as the traditional English pub it had always been. Sadly he did not keep his word and changed it almost immediately into yet another faceless wine bar. I often wonder what Gilbert and the others make of it now with its German beers and wooden benches scrawled with graffiti. Perhaps they wish they had taken up my offer to help them move on when they had the chance.

On the drive back to Wales I enjoyed a feeling of liberation. My whole being relaxed now that I was going home. The family were just as happy to be going back where they belonged. When we crossed the brow of the hill, the 'Croeso I Llandudno' sign welcomed us home. As we dipped down towards the sweeping Victorian promenade, the slopes of the spectacular Great Orme reflected in the shimmer of the ocean. The second most beautiful sight in the world.

Our girls, who were now young ladies, were glad to be in familiar surroundings, and John went up to senior school with his old school friends around him. It was like a cloud had lifted. The headlines of the local papers that dropped through our door, changed from, 'Man stabbed in McDonalds', to the wonderfully dull, 'Cake sale raises record amount for local hospice', - and it felt fantastic!

Our new house had three stories and was spacious enough to accommodate us all. Crucially there a substantial office where I could see people without the disruption of family life. The small, fragrant garden with lavender, broom and rosemary was a real treat after the city air, and the lawn was much more suitable for our ageing German shepherd and one-eyed cat.

News of my return spread around the county like a brush fire and was helped along by Tudno FM and Marcher Sound radio stations inviting me to appear. Soon Jane was back to juggling my diary in an effort to squeeze in as many people as possible. I held evenings of Clairvoyance and Psychic weekends in The Washington and St. Georges Hotel on the promenade, and was happy to conduct charity events whenever local causes approached me. I began travelling again too, even making a nostalgic return to Thimblemill Road Spiritualist Church. It was wonderful to fill those seats again and catch up with some old friends.

Away from the buzz of the city, I was free to write more and even set up a blog and a Facebook page to keep in touch with everyone. This was especially useful for those overseas who couldn't readily get to see me when they felt the need. A far cry from the early prophets who spoke from the mountain tops, the advancement of technology meant that I could now reach people on the other side of the world in the flicker of an eye. Unfortunately, in ancient times there was little distraction when someone spoke, whereas I found that words could now easily become lost within a haystack of cute cats and viral pranks. Nonetheless, people worldwide could now contact me instantly, so there were certainly some perks to living in the twenty-first century.

One summer's day I was contacted by a lady in the Isle of Man, a pretty, green island floating in the Irish Sea. She had seen me on stage a few years earlier while on holiday in Blackpool, and with a little research she succeeded in tracking me down. Her voice sounded desolate down the line as she told me her story, adding that after seeing me work she had every confidence that I could help. A few months earlier her son had left his wife after an argument and subsequently moved back home with his mother, but one afternoon she came home from work to find that he had gone missing without explanation. Days turned to weeks, and he didn't return. No one had seen or heard from him since. He had not been behaving suspiciously before he left - he just vanished. She had notified the police and was anxiously awaiting some news.

I promised to do my best for her, and explained that the easiest way for me to form a link with her son would be by holding something that belonged to him. She posted his tie to me along with a bookmark from the book he had been reading. As soon as the items arrived, I took them into my office and lit a candle. I sat in the stillness and closed my eyes as spirit drew close. Her son was not there with me, but what I was being shown was not good news.

I delayed making the call to his mother, not wanting to be the one to deliver bad news. A week went by before I was forced to face the situation. She called to find out what clues I might have for her. Jane passed the phone to me, and I lit a cigarette before I spoke. The lady's voice was soft, almost hesitant as she asked if I had found time to look at the items she sent. I felt sick to my stomach.

"Before I tell you what I saw, I want to make it clear that I do make mistakes sometimes." There was a pause before I offered my first piece of information. "I could see a green anorak." She told me with some enthusiasm how he had bought one the week before he went missing. "And a book about the history of the Isle of Man." This was the book he had been reading, from which she had taken the bookmark. "His plans had fallen through – there were difficulties with a friendship or relationship." I paused. "I'm so sorry, and I hope I am wrong, but when I held his belongings in my hands, I could feel a pain in the right side of my head and in my back. I'm afraid I picked up that he drowned. That he jumped into a rough sea."

"Don't say that! Don't say that!" she sobbed. I felt dreadful and emphasised once more that I might be mistaken. We spoke until she seemed calmer, and ended the conversation by agreeing to mutually hope that I was wrong.

Six weeks later the lady wrote to me. The police had been in touch. Her son's body had been found, washed up on the Liverpool shore. I have never been so sad to be proved right.

I am often asked what happens to a person when they take their own life. The church talks of purgatory. If life on Earth is like a day at school, then suicide can be likened to a child playing truant. To skip class and go home early before you have learned your lessons is very wrong. It is not for us to decide when we come into this world or when we leave it. That said, God is an understanding parent, and those who take themselves over are helped in the spirit world. The reasons why their actions were so wrong is explained to them, and they see the bigger picture. They are told of the lessons they were intended to learn during this life, and shown how their actions affected others.

In times of despair, it can seem an easy escape to close your eyes and make it all go away. The trouble is that your worries and heartache don't end when you die. You wake up dead, and must then move forward with the knowledge that you have only made things worse. That poor lady's son must have felt so lost and alone, and tragically now so did his mother.

On occasion, people ask me to help them find someone. From time to time I pick up snippets of information regarding missing persons or murders that appear on the news. If I was able to hold something belonging to these victims, I could probably do more, but the police do not usually take psychics seriously, (and who can blame them? Even I have encountered my fair share of crackpots), so I have never approached them unsolicited to offer my help.

In 2006, five young women were murdered over a six week period in the Ipswich area. A massive hunt was on for their killer. All the bodies were stripped naked, and two were found laid out in cruciform position. It was a horrific scene. The girls were all slim, aged nineteen to twenty-nine, and tragically were working as prostitutes to fund drug habits. As I watched the news, I strongly felt that the man they were looking for drove an unusual vehicle for a living, perhaps a tractor or a forklift, and I saw the initials S.W.

The following December a man called Steve Wright, who drove a forklift truck, was arrested by Suffolk police and subsequently convicted of the murders. There is no consolation in being right if no one is willing to listen. I did not pass the message on for fear of being accused of wasting police time. These days I occasionally tweet any information I pick up, just in case someone relevant is interested.

As the years rumbled on, everything was going well - everything that is except my health. The girls left home, settling down close to home with families of their own, and in due course they made me a very proud granddad, but increasingly I struggled with my mobility. I have been a smoker since I was fourteen, and inevitably I began to pay the price. Psychic gifts are to be used for the benefit of others, and I always knew I would never be able to heal myself. I accept this. It is only proper that the healer has no unfair advantage. Peripheral vascular disease began to affect my legs, and Chronic Obstructive Pulmonary Disease was taking my breath away. I hardly noticed them at first, but with hindsight, they stalked me for some years before they eventually brought me to my knees. Shopping trips into town became a daunting thought, so I mostly stayed at home. On family outings I would sit in a café, pretending I just didn't feel like that stroll around the fairground or market. I recall a lady once stopped me in the street and said, "Didn't you used to be David Drew?" I smiled and assured her that I still was, although I confess it struck a nerve. I ventured out less and less until it became quite normal for me to stay inside, room to room being as much as I could manage. As my mobility became more of an issue, I concentrated on writing and updating my webpage, Facebook page and blog.

Some people will tell you that time of death is predetermined at the moment of birth, but it is not, strictly speaking, the case. God gives us free will, and our actions can have an effect on our lifespan. Although there is an intended guideline at the beginning of your life for how long you will live, if you choose to smoke fifty cigarettes a day, engage in extreme sports or jump under a bus then you take the risk of hurrying the process along. Everything in this world changes, your circumstances, your health, your surroundings, but God is always the same. There is comfort in the consistency of His unchanging laws and His perpetual love.

It is not how long you live, but how you live that is important. Whenever it comes, we will all one day set out on that tremendous journey to spirit. Some will go high, and others will sink to the lowest depths, but none can avoid it. Our existence is a constant and unending cycle, as rain falls to the ground, evaporates in the sunshine and then forms a cloud. We are in the spirit world; we come to earth, and we return to spirit. Life is eternal, not just ahead but also behind us. We are spirit, we have always been, and we will always be. Often I have been accused of having the morbid job of talking about death every day. I answer that I don't talk about death, I talk about life. I talk about this life, the life before it and the life to come. We were all in spirit before we came here, and one day we will all go home.

I spoke earlier of the deep-sea diver. When he plunges into the depths of the ocean in full suit and heavy helmet, his movements are slow and restricted. I can equate this to how I feel today. For a soul to walk the earth, an outer suit is needed, which is provided in the form of our body. Incidentally, this is the only plane of existence where such a vehicle is necessary. My spirit is clothed, as is yours, in a cumbersome suit. As time goes on it becomes more and more weighty. Spirit and body are joined by the silver cord, just as the diver's air pipe links him with the surface where his movements feel light and free. When I sleep, I go up to the surface. Like the diver, I am pulled into the sunlight and transported to a place where I am whole, and every movement is not a chore.

These days I often revisit the high spirit council, where at meetings they speak of my detention, how this life has lasted longer than originally planned. I confess to underestimating the time it would take me to complete this assignment, and although disheartened, I am not yet beaten by this.

More and more, however, I do look forward to stepping out of my body for a few hours when I sleep. These days I return to my body with a weary heart, like putting on a tight pair of shoes that I cannot kick off until it is time to rest again.

This body you see before you, for what it is worth, will one day be burnt or buried, but my spirit will step out of it like throwing off an old overcoat, and it will live forever. Remember that your soul is not a separate entity, it is simply the real you. One day it will be your turn to die, and you will cast your mind back and remember my words.

Imagine your home is the most beautiful mansion, with exquisite chandeliers and magnificent gardens. Suddenly, you are told you must leave it all behind and go to live in a ghetto - a dark and dingy place. In this slum, you meet people whom you grow to love, and you get by together in your difficult surroundings as best you can. One day you receive a letter saying that you are at last able to go back to the wonderful home that you miss so desperately. You are initially excited, euphoric, but then you realise that you must go there alone, leaving the people you love behind.

This is the position in which I find myself now. I remember the beautiful place I was so reluctant to leave over sixty years ago. Before too long I know BC will gather me in his arms and carry me home. We have been together for a long, long time, and I know the story will not end there.

I remember where I came from; my chandeliers were the moon and the stars, but now that the time to go back is approaching, I have mixed feelings. Jane and my family cannot come with me. It is like winning a luxury cruise for one. I refused to cry when I was born to this world, and I will not shed a tear when I leave it.

Of course, I will be able to visit, and I know we will be together again one day, but just as sending a post card or making a phone call is not enough, when you love someone it is their physical presence you miss. As I have travelled the world Jane and I have often been physically apart, but we were always spiritually together, and so it will be in time to come. We are very lucky. I know many people who are physically together and yet spiritually they are so far apart.

We must always thank God for our trials as well as our blessings. Hardship forges our spirit like steel in a furnace. It makes us stronger, and every tear we shed in this life will one day turn into a pearl of wisdom. In the end God will decide when I must go, and I am happy to yield to His will. In fairness, I expected to pass long ago. I am still here only because I have been given detention, having not completed the work I came to do in the time frame anticipated. I am weary now. It seems the longer you carry a sword, the heavier it becomes. As I write these words, Blue Cloud stands in the doorway, arms outstretched.

After I die, my success will be measured by the success or failure of those whose lives I have touched. I have come to this world as a signpost, to show people how to live and die well, how to sail high and avoid the pits. God's natural laws are unchanging. Helping people to comprehend them is my reason for being here. The only way to change the world is to change the hearts and minds of those living in it. Understanding what happens when you die is highly enlightening, but the essence of my message is far simpler. Get this life right and the rest will take care of itself. This life is the latest step along your pathway of progression. You do not need to die before you can develop spiritually, you can strive to become more spiritual now. We each have something we can contribute to the world and its inhabitants before we pass over. We are renting our space on God's earth. Everything around us belongs to Him. The way we pay our rent is by contributing to others.

Our Earth is God's garden. He created a spectacular place for us to live out our lives among mountains, seas, trees and flowers. He provides enough food for everyone, if we would only distribute it evenly. The human race is abusing the planet and destroying the environment.

Advancements in technology and industry create pollution, modify nature and distract us from any spiritual development. Nations spend billions on nuclear, chemical and conventional weapons, while entire countries go hungry. If you lived alone in a large manor house with beautiful grounds and invited all the village children around to enjoy it, how would you feel if they pulled up all the flowers, wrecked the statues and polluted the fountains? Remember this is God's garden.

The destruction of our world is inevitable unless we change direction, and deep down we know this, but power and money speak louder to our leaders than I can. We are chasing a runaway car heading toward a cliff, and we only have a short time to avert disaster. There will however, always be an earth plane. There must always be this learning place. If the world is annihilated God will create another, and earthly life will begin all over again.

As for myself, I stand in the middle of a bridge between two worlds, shouting out messages from one side to the other. All the while souls are passing back and forth across the bridge, some coming to live a life on the earth plane, others leaving it for a life in spirit. When a child goes to school, he starts in the infant section and progresses gradually through the years until he is ready for high school. While he is there his knowledge accumulates until he is ready to graduate. It is no use trying to answer university questions when you are a junior school student. You don't need to understand the workings of high spirit now. God gives you a little knowledge at a time. Be patient and do not yearn for more knowledge until you have digested what you already have. Every morning be eager to hear what God has to teach you. All will be made clear to you, one step at a time.

You have been given this life for a purpose. If you were to pick up a book, open it at the centre pages and begin to read, the chances are the story would make no sense. This life is your middle chapter. You can't expect to understand it until you are in a position to see the whole story, and if your life has not taken you where you intended it to, remember that it was really always more about the journey than the destination.

Be aware every day of the influences around you. Both God and the devil are constantly at work. Before you act, think about who you are pleasing. It is so easy to make the wrong choice simply by not paying attention. Each evening, meditate on your day. Do you think your actions pleased God? Did you earn bricks or balloons? If you got it wrong, kick yourself, learn from it and do better tomorrow. Every day is a fresh start. It is soul destroying to see people doing the work of the devil without realising. I have now done all

I can to supply the equipment you need to avoid the bricks and win balloons.

During this life, your looks will fade, and your mind may falter, but the spirituality you have gained and the love you bear for others will remain even after you pass. As your body needs fuel, so your spirit needs sustenance in the form of spiritual knowledge. Let people remember you for what you contributed, not for how you look or how clever you are. Love and spirituality are the only things that last, the only things you can take with you, all else is trash. Make your investments well.

There is a house so beautiful, mere words could not explain-

More radiant than the sun-kissed sea, more sweet than summer rain.

Purer than a sleeping child, more wise than any sage,

These earthly beauties when compared, appear a darkened stage.

The house I speak of has no bricks, no lintels and no stove,

For it is built of truth and peace, and praise and light, and love.

And though it is within my heart, it lies far, far away.

I dare not hope that I might see my Father's house one day.

David Drew

Also by this author:

Stairway to Heaven

A reference book on life after death and psychic phenomena.

AVAILABLE IN PAPERBACK AND eBOOK

From **AMAZON.**

Printed in Great Britain
by Amazon